Power of Attorney Legislation

A STEP Global Guide

Editor
Emily Deane

Managing director
Sian O'Neill

Power of Attorney Legislation: A STEP Global Guide
is published by

Globe Law and Business Ltd
3 Mylor Close
Horsell
Woking
Surrey GU21 4DD
United Kingdom
Tel: +44 20 3745 4770
www.globelawandbusiness.com

Power of Attorney Legislation: A STEP Global Guide

ISBN 9781837230372
EPUB ISBN 9781837230389
Adobe PDF ISBN 9781837230396

Table of contents

Introduction

Emily Deane
STEP

STEP is dedicated to focusing on the significant issues that surround loss of capacity, particularly in light of a recent report stating that dementia cases are set to triple by 2050.[1] Our members are very well positioned to assist clients to put plans in place and provide safeguards should future incapacity lead to vulnerable situations, including abuse or neglect.

However, for practitioners to assist clients most effectively, they need to be supported with appropriate knowledge and legal tools. Therefore, when Globe Law and Business approached STEP to co-produce a jurisdictional comparative guide, we felt that power of attorney legislation would be a valuable and popular focus. We subsequently selected 23 STEP experts in this area to produce a Q&A chapter on the power of attorney legislation in each of their jurisdictions. The result is a clear and practical guide that will be a valuable tool to help navigate some of the existing challenges and uncertainties in relation to powers of attorney in practice.

1. The challenges

The challenges of an ageing population mean that increasing numbers of people across the globe need to plan for what would happen if they were to lose mental capacity. In England and Wales, for example, you can do this through setting up a lasting power of attorney (LPA).

However, in many countries, there is no way for people to plan ahead, as there are no legal frameworks in place to enable this. Some jurisdictions have legislation in place that is very limited and others do not have any power of attorney legislative instruments at all.

There are also issues with portability. If a jurisdiction does not have cross-border recognition, then it may mean that the legal representative appointed on the donor's behalf does not have the legal authority to make decisions in other jurisdictions. In many cases, this lack of recognition could result in delay, distress, onerous legal fees and other additional costs.

Even in countries like the United Kingdom, if you are living abroad when you lose capacity or if you have property in another country, your LPA may not be recognised in that country. This variation and the lack of consistency from one country to another is putting vulnerable people at risk of financial abuse.

As experts in inheritance and succession planning, our members have become increasingly concerned about the absence of a globally recognised and consistent form of lasting power of attorney. They shared their concerns in response to our global survey of issues in this area. The results were published in the report *Loss of Mental Capacity: A Global Perspective*.[2]

2. The Global Representative Power

The survey feedback showed that there is a clear demand for better power of attorney legislation as well as cross-border recognition and portability of powers of attorney. As a result, STEP has produced the Global Representative Power (GRP):[3] a template and benchmark for a power of attorney that will be globally recognised and portable across borders.

It will be a 'best practice' model that jurisdictions can look to when seeking or initiating new legislation where it fails to exist, or when reviewing existing provisions for efficiency, effectiveness and best practice. We are suggesting a universal approach to ensure that the recognition of an LPA or GRP is subject to the same standards and protections in any jurisdiction.

The STEP GRP was developed by a group of STEP's expert members from a range of jurisdictions – some of whom have contributed to this publication. We have sought to ensure the GRP is consistent in its language and it can be accurately and fairly applied in various jurisdictions, regardless of locally recognised legal terminology. For this reason, our use of the term 'global representative power' will encompass LPA and enduring powers of attorney (EPA) measures of protection and powers of representation. For the benefit of cross-border recognition, we recommend that jurisdictions use the terminology outlined in the GRP when considering the legislation.

Streamlining standards is also a vital feature of the GRP, as we acknowledge that the variance in cross-border situations is a cause of confusion. STEP has long supported the objectives of The Hague Convention of 2 July 2019 on the Recognition and Enforcement of Foreign Judgments in Civil or Commercial Matters in bringing uniformity to cross-border recognition of power of attorney legislation, and it has been used as a guide in this respect. This will include defining a person's decision-making ability as context specific, as well as recognising decision-making ability as fluid and rights-based.

3. What key issues is the GRP intended to solve?

The problem with power of attorney legislation is a global one. Inconsistent standards in jurisdictions means that an LPA may not be recognised in a country outside of where it was made. Many jurisdictions do not have any LPA legislative instrument at all. Other jurisdictions have LPA legislation that does not embrace the cross-border element.

The lack of cross-border recognition may mean that the legal representative appointed on the donor's behalf does not have the legal authority to make decisions in some jurisdictions. In many cases, the lack of recognition would also result in delay, distress, onerous legal fees and other additional costs. STEP believes that portability is an essential feature of any modern LPA tool. The GRP comprises a set of Guiding Principles[4] that, if adopted globally, would provide consistency and portability while protecting the rights and interests of vulnerable people.

Mitigating the financial abuse of vulnerable clients has also been a key consideration in the production of the GRP. We have discovered multiple jurisdictions without a power of attorney legal framework in place. This is especially concerning as the ever-growing, ageing global population means the risk of developing dementia and Alzheimer's disease is higher, as is the risk of financial abuse. The GRP framework endorses a number of safeguards aimed at preventing abuse which include restrictions on who is able to make or witness a GRP, who may be appointed as a representative and ensuring clarity around decision-making matters in the event of marriage or divorce. Individuals are also able to revoke their GRP while they maintain decision-making capacity.

We support additional measures to modernise the framework, including the digitisation of LPAs but only if we can be assured that

STEP is urging governments to uphold standards to ensure that people are able to express their wishes and make decisions, as is their fundamental human right. We are calling on governments to provide additional measures and safeguards for people who may face loss of capacity.

appropriate measures are in place to mitigate online and technical vulnerabilities and abuse.

4. Is STEP calling for replacement legislation?

STEP is calling for greater portability of powers in international legislation, to enable better decision-making abilities concerning financial and property matters. The GRP is not 'replacement legislation', but rather a tool for legislators who are yet to implement LPAs. The STEP model draws from the strengths of existing LPA legislation in jurisdictions such as England and Wales, which already recognises and accepts cross-border LPAs.

By introducing the GRP, we are calling for a global approach that adopts a uniformed template for LPAs, followed by the adoption of a consistent framework which can be applied in a global context to determine incapacity and impairment.

5. What are the next steps in terms of bringing GRPs into force?

STEP is urging governments to uphold standards to ensure that people are able to express their wishes and make decisions, as is their fundamental human right. We are calling on governments to provide additional measures and safeguards for people who may face loss of capacity. This includes strengthening testing of LPAs where decisions are being made in relation to a person's health outcomes.

STEP has produced the GRP, along with the Guiding Principles, in order to provoke greater international discussion around the themes of loss of capacity, while promoting power of attorney legislation that is consistent in the cross-border context. We have already engaged with certain jurisdictions to propose the benefits of implementing a more universal and cohesive legal framework and will report on our progress in due course.

6. This Special Report

STEP is dedicated to building awareness of the importance of power of attorney legislation. Powers of attorney have a crucial role to play in looking after vulnerable people, including the elderly and those with medical conditions.

It is evident that standards are inconsistent across the world. Therefore, having a comparative guide for a multitude of jurisdictions will be especially valuable for international advisers. In this Special Report, STEP members have produced Q&A chapters for their own jurisdictions that address the key questions in relation to the different types of power of attorney, protective measures, formalities, registration and portability.

It is clear from producing this Special Report that some jurisdictions have more comprehensive legislation than others. The United States has different state statutes: we were unable to cover them all and so have selected specific states to discuss. Some chapters are shorter than others – this is due to nominal legislation in place. It is interesting to note that the majority of jurisdictions do not have legislative provision for medical or health and welfare powers. There is also a range of differing approaches towards capacity assessments, formalities and registration and – not unexpectedly – very few jurisdictions recognise foreign powers.

In summary, this Special Report provides quick and informative answers to any questions that advisers might have in relation to the policy and legislation of a particular jurisdiction. Most clients have assets and property spread across jurisdictions these days and it is essential for their advisers to know how the legal framework in those places will coordinate with the client's own jurisdiction.

Notes

1 *The Lancet*, "Estimation of the global prevalence of dementia in 2019 and forecasted prevalence in 2050: an analysis for the Global Burden of Disease Study 2019", www.thelancet.com/journals/lanpub/article/PIIS2468-2667(21)00249-8/fulltext.
2 STEP, *Loss of Mental Capacity: A Global Perspective*, www.step.org/research-reports/mental-capacity.
3 STEP, Global Representative Power, www.step.org/GRP.
4 STEP, *Global Representative Power for Property and Financial Affairs*, "Guiding Principles", www.step.org/system/files/media/files/2023-11/STEP-GRP-guiding-principles.PDF.

Australia

Nour Harb
Tindall Gask Bentley Lawyers
Timothy Morton
Glass Goodwin
Leah Sewell
Chalfont Chambers

The authors have outlined the legislation applicable in the Australian Capital Territory (ACT), New South Wales, Victoria and South Australia as these are the states within their expertise.

1. Does your jurisdiction have legislation providing for powers of representation such as ordinary, continuing, enduring or lasting powers of attorney?

ACT

Yes, Powers of Attorney Act 2006 (ACT) with forms set by regulation (the 2006 Act).

New South Wales

Yes, Powers of Attorney Act 2003 (NSW) with forms set by regulations (the 2003 Act).

Victoria

Yes, Powers of Attorney Act 2014 (Vic) with forms set by regulation (the 2014 Act).

South Australia

Yes, Powers of Attorney and Agency Act 1984 (SA) (the 1984 Act).

2. When do powers of representation come into effect?

ACT

Either immediately, from a set date or event, or (in relation to enduring powers of attorney) when only the principal has impaired decision-making capacity. The commencement is set by the principal.

New South Wales

The default position is that they come into effect immediately on execution. You can also elect to defer when they come into effect generally on the provision of a medical certificate that the principal is unable to manage his or her financial affairs or when the attorney considers the principal needs assistance managing his or her affairs. Another option is also permitted, but requires specific details to be inserted or a date.

Victoria

Either immediately, when the principal ceases to have decision-making capacity (in relation to enduring powers of attorney), or from a date or when certain circumstances arise.

South Australia

Immediately upon execution, on suffering any subsequent legal incapacity or from a set date or event.

3. Does your jurisdiction have a legal test for determining mental capacity?

ACT

Yes. In respect of enduring documents there are tests for making the document and when the enduring instrument may come into force.

As to the former, this is set out at Section 17 of the 2006 Act and is included as the final schedule in the prescribed form.

As to the latter, this is set out at Section 9 of the 2006 Act.

New South Wales

No, there is no legal test. The 2003 Act is silent as to the criteria for capacity and process of assessment. However, some decisions of the Supreme Court in the Protective List have set out some guidelines – *Szozda v Szozda* [2010] NSWSC 804; *Scott v Scott* [2012] NSWSC 1541; (capacity generally: *Gibbons v Wright* (1954) 91 CLR 423).

Victoria

Yes, both to make the document and when the document may come into force. The test is the same and found in Section 4 of the 2014 Act.

South Australia

No. The 1986 Act is silent as to the criteria for capacity and the processes for the assessment of capacity in both the making of the instrument and its activation. The 1986 Act is also silent on what amounts to capacity or incapacity. Common law is reverted to, leading cases being *Banks v Goodfellow* (1871) LR11Eq 472, *Gibbons v Wright* (1954) 91 CLR 423 and *K's Statutory Will, Re* (2017) 96 NSWLR 69.

4. Can the powers of representation deal with property and finances and/or health and welfare?

ACT

Yes. The enduring instrument applies to property, personal care, medical care and medical research matters.

New South Wales

No. A power of attorney can only deal with financial and legal matters. It cannot be used to make decisions about where someone lives, what medical or dental care they receive or other personal services. A separate instrument made under the Guardianship Act 1987 (NSW) is necessary.

Victoria

Yes. The enduring instrument also applies to personal care matters but not medical care matters, which are provided for under an appointment of medical decision maker pursuant to the Medical Treatment Planning and Decisions Act 2016 (Vic).

South Australia

A valid instrument enables the donee to act on behalf of the donor in relation to legal and financial decisions. A separate instrument is required for health and lifestyle decisions, being an Advanced Care Directive.

5. Are there any other protective measures available?

ACT

You may make a heath direction and a statement of choices in relation to medical matters.

New South Wales

An appointment of enduring guardian under the Guardianship Act 1987 (NSW) to make decisions in relation to accommodation, health care and other personal services.

Victoria

You may appoint a medical decision maker and make an advance care directive.

South Australia

Pursuant to the Advance Care Directives Act 2013 (SA), you are able to make directions about medical and lifestyle decisions and appoint substitute decision makers.

Some protection is offered through Section 7 of the 1984 Act which stipulates that a donee of an enduring power of attorney must, during any period of legal incapacity of the donor, conduct him or herself with reasonable diligence to protect the interests of the donor.

6. What are the formalities of establishing a power of representation?

ACT

Two adult witnesses are required with one witness needing to be qualified to witness a statutory declaration in the ACT (the list is long but relevantly includes a legal practitioner or a justice of the peace). All witnesses must be present at the same time.

There is no process for remote witnessing at this time.

New South Wales

An enduring power of attorney must be executed before a prescribed witness who also provides the principal with a certificate stating they have explained the effect of the instrument and the person appeared to understand it. No witness is required for the attorney to sign the acceptance.

Remote witnessing under the Electronic Transactions Act 2000 (NSW) is possible.

Victoria

Two adult witnesses with no requirement that either witness have particular qualifications.

South Australia

There is a procedure for remote witnessing that requires one witness to be a special witness. There are no formal requirements in the 1984 Act as to the requirements of the instrument itself, however case law establishes that powers of attorney agreements must be in writing and either made by, or contained in, a deed.

The 1984 Act provides that to execute, the donor's signature needs to be witnessed by a witness, who must be a person authorised by law to take affidavits.

The Schedules to the 1984 Act provide the form and acceptance of a general power of attorney.

7. Is there a registration process for powers of representation?

ACT
Yes. This is required if the attorney is going to deal with real property under powers given in the instrument.

New South Wales
Yes. This is required if the attorney is going to deal with real property under the powers and it must be registered with the NSW Land Registry Services, otherwise registration is not required.

Victoria
Yes. This is required if the attorney is going to deal with real property under powers given in the instrument.

South Australia
Yes, but as above, only in relation to real property. It is registrable with the Officer of the Registrar General's office.

8. Can a power of representation be revoked or terminated (eg, in the event of marriage, divorce or death)?

ACT
The power can be revoked intentionally and unintentionally by:

- the execution of a revocation document (see Schedule 1 to the 2006 Act – prescribed form);
- the resignation by the attorney, noting approval by the ACT Civil and Administrative Tribunal is required where the principal has lost capacity;
- the terms of the instrument (Section 56);
- marriage, provided that the instrument has not been made in contemplation of marriage (Section 58);
- divorce (Section 59);
- death of the principal (Section 60);
- death of an attorney revokes the power of attorney in relation to that attorney (Section 61);
- bankruptcy or personal insolvency of the attorney, in relation to financial matters (Section 62);
- the incapacity of the attorney (Section 63);
- winding up of corporate attorney (Section 64);
- the principal not having capacity and attorneys are appointed together but not separately in relation to a matter and the power is revoked in relation to one attorney (Section 67);
- later power of attorney, to the extent of inconsistency (Section 69); or
- by order of the ACT Civil and Administrative Tribunal or the Supreme Court of the Australian Capital Territory.

New South Wales

The power can be revoked by:

- resignation of the attorney;
- revocation in writing by the principal if he or she has capacity;
- death of the attorney and/or joint attorneys unless a statement in the instrument means death of one does not terminate the other's appointment; or
- by order of NSW Civil and Administrative Tribunal or Supreme Court of New South Wales (Protective List).

Victoria

The power can be revoked by:

- execution of an instrument of revocation (Part 5, Division 2 of the 2014 Act);
- the resignation by the attorney, noting approval by the Victorian Civil and Administrative Tribunal is required where the principal has lost capacity;
- the death of the principal (Section 51);
- the death of the attorney (Section 52);
- loss of capacity of the attorney (Section 53);
- insolvency of the attorney (Section 54(1)(a));
- the attorney becoming a care worker, health or accommodation provider for the principal (Section 54(1)(b));
- the attorney for financial matters being convicted of an offence involving dishonesty (Section 54(1)(c));
- a corporate attorney being wound up or ceasing to be registered (Section 54(2)); or
- by order of the Victorian Civil and Administrative Tribunal or the Supreme Court of Victoria.

South Australia

There is no clear form of revocation within the 1984 Act. The power granted under a valid power of attorney can be revoked by:

- execution of an instrument that qualifies as a revocation;
- notice of resignation by the donee, however, if the donor has lost legal incapacity then permission of the Supreme Court of South Australia is required;
- order of the SACAT;
- loss of legal capacity of the donor (power of attorney, not enduring power of attorney);
- the incapacity of the donee;
- winding up of corporate attorney; or
- where the power conferred is conditional upon a joint appointment (two donees), the entire power is revoked if one attorney subsequently becomes legally incapacitated or dies.

9. Is the process of making and/or registering a power of representation supervised by a court or government body?

ACT
There is no supervision for making powers of attorney. The registration of powers of attorney is supervised by the ACT Land Titles Office.

New South Wales
There is no supervision for making a power of attorney.

Victoria
There is no supervision for making a power of attorney.

South Australia
There is no supervision for making a power of attorney or registrable body.

10. Is there a governmental or administrative body with oversight of the validity of a power of representation and supervision of its use?

ACT
Yes, the ACT Civil and Administrative Tribunal.

New South Wales
Yes, NSW Civil and Administrative Tribunal and Supreme Court of New South Wales (Protective List).

Victoria
Yes, the Victorian Civil and Administrative Tribunal and the Victorian Supreme Court.

South Australia
Yes, South Australian Civil and Administrative Tribunal and the South Australian Supreme Court.

11. What role do the courts in your jurisdiction have in relation to powers of representation?

ACT
The Supreme Court can hear claims against attorneys for loss where the attorneys have not complied with their obligations. All other matters are heard by the ACAT at first instance with rights of appeal to the Supreme Court of the Australian Capital Territory.

New South Wales

The Supreme Court may review a power of attorney, may appoint, vary, confirm or void the appointment of the attorney in its protective capacity. Claims may be brought in the equity division for breaches of the fiduciary duties.

Appointment of someone by the court will usually be the NSW trustee and guardian rather than a private individual.

Appointments of financial managers in NCAT will be overseen by the NSW trustee and guardian.

Victoria

Matters may be heard at first instance by the Supreme Court or VCAT.

South Australia

The Supreme Court of South Australia is the only court that has the jurisdiction to hear claims against donees and failure to comply with obligations/fiduciary obligations.

While the instrument is still live, the SACAT, with rights of appeal to the Supreme Court.

12. Are foreign powers of representation legally recognised in your jurisdiction? If so, what is the applicable legal framework?

ACT

Yes, provided they are made under the laws of another Australian state or territory. Power is limited to powers that could be validly conferred under the local legislation.

New South Wales

The 2003 Act is silent on the recognition of foreign powers of attorney, but specifically recognises powers of attorney that have been made in other states and territories of Australia, provided they have been certified as complying with that legislation.

It is unclear whether a foreign power of attorney is recognised.

Victoria

Yes, provided they are made under the laws of another Australian state or territory. Power is limited to powers that could be validly conferred under the local legislation.

South Australia

Section 14 of the 1984 Act provides for the recognition of a POA made interstate. An interstate POA has effect as if it were an enduring POA made under, and in compliance with, the 1984 Act, but only insofar as the powers it gives under the law of the State or Territory in which it was made could validly have been given by an enduring POA made under this act.

13. Has your jurisdiction ratified The Hague Convention on the International Protection of Adults 2000? If not, are there any plans for your jurisdiction to do so in the near future?

ACT
No, there are no plans to ratify.

New South Wales
No, there are no plans to ratify.

Victoria
No, there are no plans to ratify.

South Australia
No, there are no plans to ratify.

14. Is there any publicly available guidance on the law and procedure concerning powers of representation in your jurisdiction?

ACT
Some guidance is provided by the ACT Law Society and is currently being reviewed: https://actlawsociety.asn.au/for-the-public/fact-sheets/enduring-power-of-attorney. Similar information is provided by the ACT PTG: www.ptg.act.gov.au/enduring-powers-of-attorney.

New South Wales
Yes. See Justice Connect:
https://justiceconnect.org.au/resources/powers-of-attorney-in-nsw/
and the Law Society of NSW:
www.lawsociety.com.au/sites/default/files/2018-04/Enduring%20POA.pdf.

Victoria
Yes. See the Office of the Public Advocate:
www.publicadvocate.vic.gov.au/your-rights/enduring-power-of-attorney/making-a-power-of-attorney and the Victorian Government justice of the peace handbook: www.vic.gov.au/11-powers-attorney.

South Australia
South Australian forms can be downloaded from the Land Services SA website: www.landservices.com.au/ or purchased as part of a do-it-yourself kit from Service SA, or from the Legal Services Commission.

Bermuda

Claire van Overdijk KC
Carey Olsen Bermuda

1. Does your jurisdiction have legislation providing for powers of representation such as ordinary, continuing, enduring or lasting powers of attorney?

The Powers of Attorney Act 1944 (as amended in 1986) (1944 Act) provides the statutory basis for enduring powers of attorney (EPA) in Bermuda.

Section 2 of the 1944 Act provides as follows:

Execution of instruments under power of attorney

> 2 *(1) Subsections (2) and (3) shall have effect and shall be deemed always to have had effect with respect to the execution or doing of any assurance, instrument or thing under a power of attorney.*
>
> *(2) A person who is the donee of a power of attorney may, if he thinks fit, execute or do any assurance, instrument or thing in and with his own name and signature, and under his own seal (where sealing is required) by the authority of the donor of the power; and every assurance, instrument and thing so executed and done shall be as effectual in law, to all intents, as if it had been executed or done by the donee of the power in the name and with the signature and seal of the donor therefore.*

Further, Section 6 provides that:

> *[a] provision in a power of attorney expressly stating that it may be exercised during any subsequent legal incapacity of the donor is valid and effectual, subject to such conditions and restrictions, if any, as are contained therein and are not inconsistent with this Act.*

Other than the 1944 Act, the exercise of powers by an attorney under an EPA is governed by common law rules concerning the law of agency, in particular the creation of a fiduciary relationship whereby the grantor expressly authorises the attorney to act on his or her behalf when incapacitated. In this context, the rights and duties of the donor and attorney are generally construed in accordance with the terms of the EPA subject as long as they are consistent with the 1944 Act.

2. When do powers of representation come into effect?

Unless provided otherwise in the EPA, the instrument will come into full effect on the date it is signed by the donor, and it will remain in force until such time as it is revoked by the donor or until the death of the donor.

It is possible to expressly provide in the EPA that it will not come into effect until the donor's physician issues a medical certificate stating that the donor is incapable of managing his or her own affairs. Thus, while the instrument in this case is validly executed upon the signature of the donor, it does not confer any powers to the donee until a medical certificate is issued confirming the donor's incapacity.

3. Does your jurisdiction have a legal test for determining mental capacity?

Section 5 of the 1944 Act provides that:

> *'legal incapacity' means, in relation to any person, mental infirmity of such a nature as would, but for this Act, invalidate or terminate a power of attorney and 'legal capacity' shall be construed accordingly.*

No statutory definition exists in Bermuda for 'mental infirmity'. Chapter 9 of the Code of Practice Mental Health Act 1968 sets out a definition of mental capacity that closely follows Sections 2 and 3 of the Mental Capacity Act 2005 as adopted in England and Wales. In this context, the first stage is to assess whether the person has an impairment of the mind or brain, or a disturbance in the functioning of the mind or brain. This is followed by the second step, which is to ascertain whether the impairment or disturbance in the functioning of the mind or brain means the person is unable to make the decision in question at the time it needs to be made.

In determining whether the person has the ability to make the relevant decision, four criteria need to be met. The person must have:

- a general understanding of what decision he or she needs to make and why;
- a general understanding of the likely consequences of making or not making the decision;
- the ability to understand, retain use and weigh up the information relevant to the decision; and
- the ability to communicate his or her decision (by talking, using sign language or any other means).

This definition of mental capacity does not, however, appear in the Mental Health Act 1968 (1968 Act), and while it is not legally binding, it is instructive and helpful as guidance on the assessment of mental capacity in all contexts, including those concerning the validity and use of an EPA.

4. Can the powers of representation deal with property and finances and/or health and welfare?

An EPA only deals with a donor's property and finances, and does not extend to decisions regarding the donor's health and welfare. There is presently no legal framework in place in Bermuda for making health and welfare decisions through a power of representation. It is, however, common practice to make a 'living will' when undergoing financial planning. Such a document is usually appended to an EPA or a will expressing the donor's wishes with regards to health and welfare decisions in the event of incapacity. While such a document does not have any legal effect, it is a useful record of the individual's wishes upon incapacity, which can offer instructive guidance to family members and professionals when making decisions on the person's behalf.

5. Are there any other protective measures available?

Where a person has not made an EPA and has become mentally incapacitated, the Supreme Court has jurisdiction pursuant to Part IV of the 1968 Act to make decisions on behalf of that individual (referred to as the 'patient') or to appoint a receiver to make decisions on the patient's behalf.

The 1968 Act is complemented by the Mental Health (Patient's Property) Rules 1970, which sets out the procedural rules for applications made pursuant to Part IV of the 1968 Act. Part IV gives the Supreme Court power to make property and financial decisions on behalf of a patient, but does not extend to making decisions in relation to a patient's health and welfare.

An EPA must be executed in the presence of a witness who is not the attorney or the attorney's spouse. It is also accepted practice in Bermuda that an EPA is executed as a deed, and the donor must have the requisite legal capacity to carry out this act.

Section 51 of the 1968 Act confers power on the Supreme Court to do all things appearing necessary or expedient in respect of the patient's property and affairs for the maintenance or benefit of the patient, the patient's family, and for obligations and or affairs the patient would perform were the patient mentally well. Powers are further conferred for handling the interests of the patient's possible creditors.

Section 52 of the 1968 Act empowers the Supreme Court to make decisions related to the patient's property and affairs as follows:

- control;
- sale, exchange, charging, or other disposition;
- acquisition of any property;
- settlement or gifts (subject to Section 51);
- continuing business or trade;
- dissolution of partnerships;
- contractual performance;
- legal proceedings;
- reimbursement for purposes of debt, maintenance, or other benefit; and
- the exercise of any power vested in the patient whether beneficially or as guardian or trustee, or otherwise.

Finally, Section 54 sets out the court's power to appoint a receiver in respect of the patient's property and affairs.

6. What are the formalities of establishing a power of representation?

An EPA must be executed in the presence of a witness who is not the attorney or the attorney's spouse. It is also accepted practice in Bermuda that an EPA is executed as a deed, and the donor must have the requisite legal capacity to carry out this act.

Where more than one donee is appointed, the instrument should specify whether the donees are appointed to act on a joint basis or on a joint and several basis. If they are appointed jointly, the donees must make joint decisions, and cannot act unilaterally. Further, in the event that one of the joint donees dies, the instrument will automatically terminate.

Donees appointed on a joint and several basis may make decisions unilaterally without the involvement of their co-donee. Further, if one of the donees dies, the instrument will not terminate and the other donee is able to continue in his or her role. Joint and several powers are most frequently used when it is expected that one or more of the donees may be unable to act because of absence, ill health or death.

Substitute donees can also be provided for in the instrument should one of the donees die, become unable to act or wishes to disclaim his or her appointment. This can provide a practical solution to avoid the termination of an EPA where donees are not appointed on a joint and several basis.

7. Is there a registration process for powers of representation?
There is no legal requirement in Bermuda to register an EPA in order for it to be effective. However, ordinary powers of attorney and EPAs can be registered voluntarily in order to provide public notification that the power exists. This is done by filing the power with the Registry General, which is the government body responsible for the legal recording of documents, including deeds.

8. Can a power of representation be revoked or terminated (ie, in the event of marriage, divorce or death)?
An EPA can be revoked in two instances, the first being when the donor has regained capacity to revoke the EPA, and the other being upon the death of the donor. Upon revocation of an EPA, the powers of the donee to handle the donor's affairs cease. Thereafter, the executors of the deceased will take over the administration of the deceased's affairs from the donee or receiver.

Furthermore, Section 9 of the 1944 Act provides that an EPA becomes invalid and of no effect on the exercise of the Supreme Court of any of its powers under Part IV of the 1968 Act.

9. Is the process of making and/or registering a power of representation supervised by a court or government body?
The process of making and/or registering a power of representation is not supervised by the court or by a government body. The government announced in 2020 that it would establish the Office of the Public Guardian (OPG) to provide independent services and support for seniors, children and other vulnerable persons in circumstances where they are unable to make decisions for themselves in the management of their health, financial or legal affairs. The OPG has since been established but its remit does not currently extend to the execution or supervision of EPAs, or their registration.

10. Is there a governmental or administrative body with oversight of the validity of a power of representation and supervision of its use?
Any issues with regard to the validity of an EPA is within the jurisdiction of the Supreme Court and falls to be decided pursuant to principles of common law.

Further, any suspicions of financial and/or physical abuse of a vulnerable senior can be filed with the government's Ageing and Disability Services, in accordance with the Senior Abuse Register Act 2008. That office is empowered to conduct the necessary investigations to ensure that such abuse is addressed appropriately.

11. What role do the courts in your jurisdiction have in relation to powers of representation?

While there is no compulsory registration process for EPAs in Bermuda, Section 10 of the 1944 Act provides that any person who has an interest in the estate of an incapacitated donor of an EPA may apply to the Supreme Court for an order to require the donee to render accounts for any or all transactions involving the exercise of his or her powers under the instrument.

Further, Section 11 of the 1944 Act similarly provides that any such interested person may apply to the Supreme Court for an order substituting another suitable person for the attorney named in the instrument.

Further, as stated above, the Supreme Court may determine any dispute regarding the validity of an EPA.

12. Are foreign powers of representation legally recognised in your jurisdiction? If so, what is the applicable legal framework?

There are no statutory provisions or rules in place governing the use of foreign powers of representation in Bermuda. Nor are there any reported decisions from the courts providing legal guidance on the issue. In the circumstances, one must look to common law and conflicts of law principles to determine the use of foreign powers of representation.

In this context, a distinction needs to be made between: (i) the internal relationship between donor and donee; and (ii) the external relationship between donor and third party through the agency created by the EPA.

The internal relationship between donor and donee is governed by the law governing that internal relationship (ie, the law of the jurisdiction in which the foreign power was made). As a general proposition, it is suggested that, if a foreign power of representation fully complies with the requirements in the jurisdiction in which it is made, then, to the extent the powers it gives could validly have been given by an EPA made under the 1944 Act, the power is likely to be treated as if it were a valid EPA under Bermuda law.

The relationship between principal and third party on the other hand is governed by the law governing the external relationship, namely the laws of Bermuda as the jurisdiction where it is intended to use the power. Thus, in the likely event that a financial institution in Bermuda is unwilling to accept the use of a foreign power of attorney, an affidavit confirming that the validity of the foreign power under the relevant foreign law should be provided, along with an explanation of the reasons for seeking to use the instrument in Bermuda. Alternatively, it may be necessary to seek an order from the Supreme Court confirming the validity of the EPA.

13. Has your jurisdiction ratified The Hague Convention on the International Protection of Adults 2000? If not, are there any plans for your jurisdiction to do so in the near future?

The Hague Convention on the International Protection of Adults 2000 has not been ratified by the United Kingdom in respect of Bermuda as a British Overseas Territory. Nor is there any indication that the United Kingdom intends to ratify the convention in respect of Bermuda in the near future.

14. Is there any publicly available guidance on the law and procedure concerning powers of representation in your jurisdiction?

Publicly available guidance is available as follows:

- Powers of Attorney Act 1944 (as amended);
- Mental Health Act 1968 (as amended);
- Mental Health (Patient's Property) Rules 1970;
- Mental Health Act 1968 Code of Practice: www.gov.bm/sites/default/files/Mental_Health_Code%20of%20Practice%202021_artwork%20credit.pdf; and
- *Guide to Powers of Attorney in Bermuda,* published by Appleby Bermuda: www.yumpu.com/en/document/read/29769528/guide-to-powers-of-attorney-in-bermuda-appleby.

British Virgin Islands

Fraser Allister
Andrew Miller
Bedell Cristin

1. Does your jurisdiction have legislation providing for powers of representation such as ordinary, continuing, enduring or lasting powers of attorney?
The only statutory regulation of powers of attorney is Part VI of the Conveyancing and Law of Property Act 1961.

There is no legislation providing for continuing, enduring or lasting powers of attorney.

2. When do powers of representation come into effect?
Subject to the express terms of a power of attorney, the power and authority of the donee commences immediately upon grant.

3. Does your jurisdiction have a legal test for determining mental capacity?
The capacity to grant a power of attorney is the same as the capacity of the donor to make the contract or do the act which the donee is authorised to make or do.

Under the Mental Health Act 2014, 'mental disorder' means:

- a health condition that is characterised by:
  - alterations in thinking, mood or behaviour; or a combination

of alterations in thinking, mood or behaviour, associated with distress, impaired functioning, or distress and impaired functioning; or
- a health condition arising from the use of a narcotic drug or substance.

It is generally considered that the test for capacity, as established in the case of *Banks v Goodfellow*,[1] applies both to testamentary capacity and to the exercise of powers. That test is that the relevant person must be able to:

- understand the nature of the relevant act and its effects;
- understand the extent of the property being disposed of by the relevant act; and
- understand the legal claims that may result.

4. Can the powers of representation deal with property and finances and/or health and welfare?
A donor may only grant powers in respect of property and finances under a power of attorney.

5. Are there any other protective measures available?
If an individual is incapable of managing or administering his or her property and affairs by reason of a mental disorder, the High Court has broad powers under Part IX of the Mental Health Act 2014.

Such powers include doing or ensuring the doing of things as appear necessary or expedient for:

- the maintenance or other benefit of the individual or members of the individual's family;
- making provision for other persons or purposes for whom or which the individual might be expected to provide if the individual were not suffering from a mental disorder; or
- administering the individual's affairs.

Further, at the instance of the Attorney General, the High Court may make orders and give directions and authorisations as it considers appropriate for the purposes described above for, among other things:

- the control and management of any property of the individual, with or without the transfer or vesting of property or the payment into court of securities;
- the sale, exchange, charging or other disposition of or dealing with any property of the individual;
- the acquisition of any property in the name or on behalf of the individual;

- the settlement of any property of the individual, or the gift of any property of the individual to any person or for any purposes mentioned in the first two bullet points of the previous bullet list;
- the execution of a will for the individual;
- the carrying on by a suitable person of any profession, trade or business of the individual;
- the dissolution of a partnership of which the individual is a member;
- the carrying out of any contract entered into by the individual;
- the conduct of legal proceedings in the name of the individual or on the individual's behalf including any order, direction or authority to present a petition in the name or on behalf of the individual for:
  - divorce or nullity of marriage;
  - presumption of death or dissolution of marriage; or
  - judicial separation; or
- the exercise of any power vested in the individual beneficially or as a guardian, trustee or otherwise, including a power to consent.

6. What are the formalities of establishing a power of representation?

There are no formal requirements to make a power of attorney, although the donor will not be able to execute a deed on behalf of the donor unless the power of attorney itself were made as a deed.

In practice, powers of attorney are commonly executed as deeds and such execution is witnessed for evidential reasons.

7. Is there a registration process for powers of representation?

A power of attorney may, but need not, be registered in the Register of Deeds pursuant to the Registration and Records Act 1881.

8. Can a power of representation be revoked or terminated (ie, in the event of marriage, divorce or death)?

Where a power of attorney is not otherwise irrevocable, the agency of the donee is terminated:

- by revocation of the donor;
- by renunciation by the donee;
- on the death, bankruptcy or mental incapacity of the donor;
- by the death or mental incapacity of the donee;
- at the end of a period specified in the power of attorney; and
- by the completion of the purpose, if any, for which the power of attorney was granted.

9. Is the process of making and/or registering a power of representation supervised by a court or government body?
No.

10. Is there a governmental or administrative body with oversight of the validity of a power of representation and supervision of its use?
No.

11. What role do the courts in your jurisdiction have in relation to powers of representation?
A power of attorney creates an agency between the donor, as principal, and donee, as agent. The donee owes duties, including fiduciary duties, to his or her donor. The donor has all contractual and other remedies available in respect of such duties.

Third parties may enforce claims against principals and agents.

12. Are foreign powers of representation legally recognised in your jurisdiction? If so, what is the applicable legal framework?
Common law conflict of laws rules govern the recognition of foreign powers of representation.

13. Has your jurisdiction ratified The Hague Convention on the International Protection of Adults 2000? If not, are there any plans for your jurisdiction to do so in the near future?
No.

14. Is there any publicly available guidance on the law and procedure concerning powers of representation in your jurisdiction?
No.

Notes

1 (1869–70) LR 5 QB 549; [1870] 7 WLUK 15.

Canada

Ian Lebane
TD Wealth

1. Does your jurisdiction have legislation providing for powers of representation such as ordinary, continuing, enduring or lasting powers of attorney?

Canada is a federation comprising 10 provinces and three self-governing territories. Each has a legislature, an executive and a judicial arm of government. That said, the Canadian federation is generally regarded as quite decentralised, especially when it comes to 'property and civil rights', which, constitutionally, falls into the legislative domain of the provinces and territories.

In Canada, the law is made up of statutes passed by the legislature (both federal and provincial/territorial legislation), as well as precedents arising from decided cases over many years that have applied the principles of the common law and equity. In the province of Quebec, however, the foundation is quite different since the laws in that province reflect a civil law tradition. The law surrounding the representation of incapable individuals in that province reflect this and differ markedly from the other (common law) jurisdictions and, unless otherwise indicated, the comments below are not reflective of the unique set of rules and principles relating to incapable persons in Quebec.

The legal regime pertaining to powers of representation is governed by principles of common law (eg, contract, agency), equity (fiduciary law), together with a comprehensive statutory regime in each of the 13 Canadian sub-national jurisdictions. In Canada, while nomenclature does differ, the most common term for the documents created by grantors for others to exercise authority on their behalf are powers of attorney and will be referred to below as a 'POA' with the representative described as the 'attorney'. In Ontario, for example, the legislation contemplates two documents permitting a representative to act on behalf of an incapable grantor: for property decisions the document is called a Continuing Power of Attorney for Property (CPOA); and for health and welfare decisions the document is known as a Power of Attorney for Personal Care (POAPC). Each jurisdiction has its own statute governing POAs, which generally operate to supplement and often override the operation of the common law. For example, historically, under agency law, the authority under a POA terminated upon the incapacity of the grantor. The modern statutes in all the Canadian jurisdictions now provide that a POA can be drafted to survive the incapacity of the grantor. These statutes also provide, in a variety of ways depending on the jurisdiction, for individuals who have lost capacity to appoint someone else to make decisions about their health and welfare. For the purposes of this chapter, the legislative scheme in Ontario – by far Canada's most populous common law jurisdiction – will be used as a representative framework for the detailed comments that follow. The other common law jurisdictions are substantially similar, but practitioners must, of course, consult the relevant legislation in the jurisdiction in which the grantor resides.[1]

2. When do powers of representation come into effect?

A CPOA will generally be effective upon execution and delivery to the attorney(s), although it is open to the grantor to articulate conditions that must be fulfilled (typically, proof of a loss of capacity) before the POA is operative. A POAPC, on the other hand, is only effective when the grantor is incapable of personal care. A CPOA can be effective immediately upon execution and delivery to the named attorney; or it can contain conditions as to time, location of grantor (eg, operating when grantor is out of Canada); or it can be made conditional on the grantor becoming incapable – often colloquially known as a 'springing' CPOA.

The challenge with the latter is that many find it more cumbersome to use since typically proof of incapacity must be furnished to financial institutions and others before transactions will be permitted. There is one solution that has found favour, which balances ease of use with the understandable desire of grantors to not bestow attorneys with power over their property when the grantor remains capable. That approach is to execute a CPOA with no restrictions (ie, effective immediately) but to lodge the CPOA with a trusted third party like a lawyer who would release it to the attorney at the party's discretion.

The criteria for release will often be set by the grantor as part of an escrow agreement or perhaps a less formal letter arrangement depending upon the relationship the grantor has with the third party. A POAPC, conversely, can only ever be in effect where the grantor is incapable of personal care.

3. Does your jurisdiction have a legal test for determining mental capacity?

Mental capacity in Canada is decision-specific and there is a presumption that a person has capacity unless it is established that he or she lacks capacity,[2] and case law and legislation are both in place setting out the correct test of mental capacity. The test for incapacity in the context of managing property under the Substitute Decisions Act provides that:

> *A person is incapable of managing property if the person is not able to understand information that is relevant to making a decision in the management of his or her property, or is not able to appreciate the reasonably foreseeable consequences of a decision or lack of decision.*[3]

Conversely, there is a different standard governing the ability of a grantor to make a CPOA. The Substitute Decisions Act provides that:

> *A person is capable of giving a CPOA if he or she,*
>
> *(a) knows what kind of property he or she has and its approximate value;*
>
> *(b) is aware of obligations owed to his or her dependants;*
>
> *(c) knows that the attorney will be able to do on the person's behalf anything in respect of property that the person could do if capable, except make a will, subject to the conditions and restrictions set out in the power of attorney;*
>
> *(d) knows that the attorney must account for his or her dealings with the person's property;*
>
> *(e) knows that he or she may, if capable, revoke the continuing power of attorney;*
>
> *(f) appreciates that unless the attorney manages the property prudently its value may decline; and*
>
> *(g) appreciates the possibility that the attorney could misuse the authority given to him or her.*[4]

Every Canadian jurisdiction has legal mechanisms allowing an applicant to ask the court to be appointed guardian of the property or person of an incapable individual. In addition, all jurisdictions also have a governmental agency that intervenes when an incapable person is in need of protection.

It is important to note that the legislation specifically provides that a grantor can be capable of giving a CPOA pursuant to the above criteria even if the grantor is incapable of managing property at the time of execution. In other words, the test for capability of managing property is different, and higher, than the test for capability of giving a CPOA.[5]

In the case of a POAPC, the test for incapacity under the Substitute Decisions Act provides that:

> *A person is incapable of personal care if the person is not able to understand information that is relevant to making a decision concerning his or her own health care, nutrition, shelter, clothing, hygiene or safety, or is not able to appreciate the reasonably foreseeable consequences of a decision or lack of decision.*[6]

And the legislation provides that a person is capable of giving a POAPC if the person:

> *(a) has the ability to understand whether the proposed attorney has a genuine concern for the person's welfare; and*
>
> *(b) appreciates that the person may need to have the proposed attorney make decisions for the person.*[7]

And, as with the CPOA above, the legislation specifically provides that a grantor can be capable of giving a POAPC pursuant to the above criteria even if the grantor is incapable of personal care at the time of execution.[8]

4. Can the power of representation deal with property and finances and/or health and welfare?

Yes, see answer to question 1, above.

5. Are the any other protective measures available?

Every Canadian jurisdiction has legal mechanisms allowing an applicant to ask the court to be appointed guardian of the property or person of an incapable individual. In addition, all jurisdictions also have a governmental agency that intervenes when an incapable person is in need of protection.[9] The Office of the Public Guardian and Trustee (PGT) can be the guardian as a last resort if circumstances are such that no appropriate individual is able to assume – or continue in – the role.

6. What are the formalities of establishing a power of representation?

For a POA in Ontario to be valid after the incapacity of the grantor, it must comply with certain legislative formalities contained in the

Substitute Decisions Act.[10] A key requirement is that it must be executed in the presence of two adult witnesses. As a result of the COVID-19 pandemic, the relevant legislation was amended to allow POAs to be signed and remotely witnessed, in counterparts. These provisions have since been made permanent and some of the other Canadian jurisdictions have similarly amended their legislation. Persons disqualified from being witnesses for either a CPOA or POAPC include: the attorney, the attorney's spouse or partner, the grantor's spouse or partner, and a child of the grantor. Non-compliance with the above can be cured by the court on application if it determines that it is in the interests of the grantor (or, in the case of a CPOA, the grantor or the grantor's dependants) to do so.

7. Is there a registration process for powers of representation?
No.

8. Can a power of representation be revoked or terminated (ie, in the event of marriage, divorce or death)?
A CPOA is terminated:

(a) when the attorney dies, becomes incapable of managing property or resigns, unless,

(i) another attorney was named jointly (unless the CPOA provides otherwise), or

(ii) the CPOA provides for the substitution of another person and that person is able and willing to act;

(b) REPEALED: 1996, c. 2, s. 8 (2);

(c) when the court appoints a guardian of property for the grantor;

(d) when the grantor executes a new CPOA, unless the grantor provides that there shall be multiple CPOAs;

(e) when the CPOA is revoked;

(f) when the grantor dies.[11]

A POAPC is terminated:

(a) when the attorney dies, becomes incapable of personal care or resigns, unless,

(i) another attorney was named jointly (unless the POAPC provides otherwise), or

(ii) the POAPC provides for the substitution of another person and that person is able and willing to act;

(b) when the court appoints a guardian for the grantor;

(c) when the grantor executes a new power of attorney for personal care, unless the grantor provides that there shall be multiple powers of attorney for personal care;

(d) when the power of attorney is revoked.[12]

9. Is the process of making and/or registering a power of representation supervised by a court or government body?
The process of making a POA is not supervised in any way. In the province of Quebec only, the equivalent of a POA is known as a 'protection mandate', where the grantor is the 'mandator' and the attorney is referred to as the 'mandatary'. In Quebec, before the mandatary can use the mandate, it must be validated by a Quebec court in a process known as homologation. In the rest of Canada there is no registration process required following execution of a POA.

10. Is there a governmental or administrative body with oversight of the validity of a power of representation and supervision of its use?
No. In Canada, oversight rests with the courts as per the question following.

11. What role do the courts in your jurisdiction have in relation to powers of representation?
Attorneys are fiduciaries and must always act in the best interests of the incapable grantor. The courts in the jurisdiction where the grantor resides have the power to sanction, remove and replace attorneys, or impose other remedies as they deem fit. The intervention of the court can be sought by any interested party, on application, with notice to the proper parties. Court intervention to deal with an attorney acting improperly can also be sought by a government agency tasked with responsibility for incapable individuals.[13]

12. Are foreign powers of representation legally recognised in your jurisdiction? If so, what is the applicable legal framework?
Every Canadian jurisdiction recognises foreign powers of representation although there are some subtle variations among jurisdictions as to how that principle is implemented. In Ontario, the Substitute Decisions Act provides that a POA is valid (whether executed inside or outside Ontario) if at the time of its execution it complied with the internal law of the place where:

- the power of attorney was executed;
- the grantor was then domiciled; or
- the grantor then had his or her habitual residence.[14]

13. Has your jurisdiction ratified The Hague Convention on the International Protection of Adults 2000? If not, are there any plans for your jurisdiction to do so in the near future?

No Canadian jurisdiction has ratified the convention nor are there any plans to do so in the near future.

14. Is there any publicly available guidance on the law and procedure concerning powers of representation in your jurisdiction?

Yes. For instance, in Ontario, the government maintains web pages describing what a CPOA and POAPC are and the main page contains a link to the PGT as well as a kit and other tools for members of the public to make a POA themselves: www.ontario.ca/page/make-power-attorney.

Notes

1 In Ontario, the statute is the Substitute Decisions Act 1992, SO 1992, c 30.
2 *Ibid*, Section 2.
3 *Ibid*, Section 6.
4 *Ibid*, Section 8(1).
5 *Ibid*, Section 9.
6 *Ibid*, Section 45.
7 *Ibid*, Section 47(1).
8 *Ibid*, Section 47(2).
9 In Ontario, this agency is known as the Office of the Public Guardian and Trustee.
10 Substitute Decisions Act 1992.
11 *Ibid*, Section 12.
12 *Ibid*, Section 53.
13 PGT (n 9).
14 Substitute Decisions Act 1992, Section 85(1).

Cayman Islands

Anthony Partridge
Ogier

1. Does your jurisdiction have legislation providing for powers of representation such as ordinary, continuing, enduring or lasting powers of attorney?

The Powers of Attorney Act (1996 Revision) (PAA) provides for ordinary powers of attorney (ordinary power of attorney).

The Registered Land Act (2018 Revision) (RLA) provides for powers of attorney relating to the disposal of any interest in land (land power of attorney).

The Health Care Decisions Act (2022 Revision) (HCDA) provides for health care advance directives and proxy appointments.

Consultations are underway to implement an Enduring Powers of Attorney Act to provide for enduring powers of attorney.

The Companies Act (2023 Revision) (CA) provides for the appointment of a person either generally or in respect of a specific matter to execute deeds or instruments under seal on its behalf.

2. When do powers of representation come into effect?

An ordinary power of attorney comes into effect on the date of execution or as otherwise set out in the power of attorney.

A land power of attorney comes into effect on execution and registration with the Registrar of Lands.

A proxy appointment takes effect following the execution of a directive and proxy appointment and only during any period in which the directive-maker is mentally incompetent.

3. Does your jurisdiction have a legal test for determining mental capacity?

There is no legal test for capacity under Cayman Islands legislation and issues of capacity therefore fall to be determined under common law principles.

The leading case which sets out the test for legal capacity in the Cayman Islands is the decision of *In the Matter of a trust known as the O Trust*.[1] The test is twofold:

- the essential requirements for establishing capacity, which will usually be the same from case to case; and
- how the test should be applied from case to case depending on the circumstances.

The test for establishing capacity, which applies to the making of wills and the exercise of any other impugned power, is the English common law test applied in relation to the execution of wills in *Hoff v Atherton*[2] which requires that "for a juristic act to be valid, the person performing it should have the mental capacity ... to understand the nature and effect of that particular act" and to make a will "the law requires what is always referred to as testamentary capacity ... proof of the capacity to understand certain important matters relating to the Will".

These "matters" were set out in *Banks v Goodfellow*:[3]

> *It is essential ... that a testator shall understand the nature of his act and its effects; shall understand the extent of the property of which he is disposing; shall be able to comprehend and appreciate the claims to which he ought to give effect ...*

The second limb is more complex, but ultimately issues such as the standard of proof, the extent of understanding required and whether there was understanding at the time of the execution of a relevant instrument, will depend on the circumstances of the case.

It should be noted that 'mental impairment' and 'serious mental illness' are defined in the Mental Health Act (2023 Revision), for the purpose of that act.

4. Can the powers of representation deal with property and finances and/or health and welfare?

There is no legislative restriction on the matters covered by an ordinary power of attorney, except those covered by the RLA. The legislation states that the power confers on the donee(s) authority to do on behalf of the donor anything that he or she can lawfully do by an attorney. Case law imposes a number of specific limits on the powers that can be delegated to an attorney. In particular, an ordinary power of attorney is only effective while the donor has capacity, meaning it would not apply to health care decisions following incapacity.

A land power of attorney is limited to the disposal of an interest in land.

A proxy appointment deals with health and welfare matters only as covered in the donor's directive. There are some limitations on what provisions are effective. The following are some of the wishes of a donor which would have no effect:

- something unlawful, including euthanasia or assisted suicide;
- something that would cause a registered practitioner to breach a professional standard or code of conduct; or
- refusal of mental health treatment.

The impact of an ineffective provision is simply that this wish of the donor is ignored.

5. Are there any other protective measures available?

Under the Grand Court Act (2015 Revision) the Cayman court can appoint a guardian for a person and the estate of a person of unsound mind or suffering from mental illness.

Under the Mental Health Act (2023 Revision), the Cayman court generally has wide powers to deal with the property and affairs of persons suffering, or suspected to be suffering, from a serious mental illness or mental impairment, or persons over whom the court has appointed a guardian and who were found to be incapable of managing their own affairs.

6. What are the formalities of establishing a power of representation?

An ordinary power of attorney must be executed as a deed or as an instrument under seal by, or by the direction and in the presence of, the donor of the power. Two other persons must be present as witnesses at the signing and must attest the instrument.

The CA requires that an instrument which is required to be made by deed or under seal (which would include an ordinary power of attorney) may be made by instrument:

- sealed with any seal of the company; or
- executed on behalf of the company by any person acting under the express or implied authority of the company and which is either expressed to be executed as, or makes clear on its face is intended to be, a deed or instrument under seal.

The CA also provides for the appointment of an attorney to execute deeds or instruments under seal on its behalf otherwise than by deed or instrument under seal, but states that a person so appointed will not constitute a donee of a power under the PAA.

To establish a directive and proxy appointment a person must be 18 or older and mentally competent to make a directive. The form in the schedule to the HCDA must be completed by or on behalf of the directive-maker and must be signed by the directive-maker in the presence of two adult witnesses who must both also sign the form. At least one of the witnesses must be a doctor, who will witness after having: (1) assessed the directive-makers competency to sign; (2) ensured the directive is being signed voluntarily; and (3) ensured that the directive-maker has been told about the directive's nature and consequences.

A land power of attorney must be completed in the prescribed form and executed by all persons shown by the register to be proprietors of the interest affected and by all other parties to the instrument, unless the registrar directs otherwise. The persons executing the instrument must appear before the registrar (or other prescribed person) accompanied by a witness for the purpose of establishing their identity. The registrar will then complete a certificate to the effect that the person signed the instrument before them. The verification step may be dispensed with by the registrar in limited circumstances. The original power of attorney is then certified by the registrar and is filed.

7. Is there a registration process for powers of representation?
There is no registration process for an ordinary power of attorney or a heath care proxy.

There is a registration requirement for a land power of attorney. Registration is via Form RL 20 which should be submitted to the Lands and Survey Department together with the prescribed registration fee and stamp duty.

8. Can a power of representation be revoked or terminated (ie, in the event of marriage, divorce or death)?

An ordinary power of attorney or a land power of attorney is usually revoked on death, bankruptcy or incapacity of the donor or the death or incapacity of the donee, except in very limited circumstances. Both powers of attorney can also be revoked by the donor of the power except again in limited circumstances.

Some of the circumstances in which an ordinary power of attorney cannot be revoked by the donor without the consent of the donee are on death, incapacity or bankruptcy of the donor, where the power is expressed to be irrevocable and is given to secure a proprietary interest of the donee of the power, or the performance of an obligation owed to the donee.

The Registrar of Lands can also revoke land powers of attorney in certain circumstances.

A directive appointing a proxy can be revoked by a mentally competent directive-maker. The revocation must be in writing and must be signed and dated. The making of a subsequent directive also revokes any earlier directive made by the same directive-maker. The ethics committee under the HCDA can also revoke a directive and proxy appointment in certain circumstances.

9. Is the process of making and/or registering a power of representation supervised by a court or government body?

The process of making an ordinary power of attorney or a proxy appointment is not supervised.

The execution and registration of a land power of attorney is supervised by the Registrar of Lands.

10. Is there a governmental or administrative body with oversight of the validity of a power of representation and supervision of its use?

The ethics committee under the HCDA can revoke a directive and proxy appointment in certain circumstances.

The Registrar of Lands oversees the filing of and can revoke land powers of attorney in certain circumstances.

Otherwise, there are no governmental or administrative bodies with oversight of any of the powers of attorney.

11. What role do the courts in your jurisdiction have in relation to powers of representation?

The Cayman courts have jurisdiction for matters arising in relation to the HCDA including the competency of an adult and validity or a directive or proxy appointment. The Cayman courts will also hear appeals from the ethics committee in relation to the revocation of directives and proxy appointments.

The Cayman courts have jurisdiction to hear matters relating to the RLA which includes land powers of attorney and to hear appeals from decisions of the Registrar of Lands in relation to land powers of attorney.

12. Are foreign powers of representation legally recognised in your jurisdiction? If so, what is the applicable legal framework?

There is no automatic recognition in the Cayman Islands of foreign ordinary powers of attorney or foreign land powers of attorney and therefore the common law principles on conflict of laws in relation to agency will apply.

Particular consideration should be given to the fact that the PAA requires that an ordinary power of attorney is executed as a deed or as an instrument under seal. If a foreign ordinary power of attorney is not exercised as a deed and the act for which the donee intends to use the power is the execution of a deed on behalf of the donor, this may not be a valid use of the power if the law applicable to the execution of the deed is the Cayman Islands. This is due to the fact that under common law a person cannot authorise another to execute a deed for them except under an authority created by deed.

In relation to companies, the CA states that an instrument to be governed by the laws of the Islands which is executed by an overseas company is, and is to be treated as, a deed or instrument under seal if it is executed as set out above and it is executed in conformity with the requirements of the laws of the jurisdiction in which the company was formed or incorporated and its memorandum or articles of association or other constitutional documents.

Instruments which have, or include, similar functions to a directive and/or proxy appointment will be recognised in the Cayman Islands if they were made under the law of one of the following jurisdictions:

- United Kingdom;
- Australia;
- Canada;
- South Africa;

- New Zealand;
- Jamaica;
- United States; or
- a jurisdiction that is a member state of the European Union under the Treaty on European Union signed in Maastricht on 7 February 1992.

Such instruments will have effect for persons in the Cayman Islands as if they had been made under the HCDA and the functions of registered practitioners and proxies are those under the HCDA and not the laws of the jurisdiction under which the instrument was made. This applies despite the other jurisdictions' laws or the provisions of the instrument itself, except in the case of the law of England to the extent it applies to the Cayman Islands.

Also, a provision in such an instrument has no effect if: (a) it requires a registered practitioner to provide a person with any particular type of health care, except the denial of particular or any health care; or (b) it is a barred provision, for example, it is unlawful. This does not apply for a law of England to the extent it applies to the Cayman Islands.

A Cayman court cannot currently recognise an enduring or lasting power of attorney from another jurisdiction because it is not a procedure known to Cayman law. However, the Cayman courts may instead exercise jurisdiction over the property of a mentally incapacitated person situated in the Cayman Islands and appoint a guardian for such a person. It may find it appropriate to appoint the attorneys under the foreign enduring or lasting power of attorney as guardians.

13. Has your jurisdiction ratified The Hague Convention on the International Protection of Adults 2000? If not, are there any plans for your jurisdiction to do so in the near future?
The Cayman Islands has not ratified The Hague Convention on the International Protection of Adults 2000. There are no known plans to do so.

14. Is there any publicly available guidance on the law and procedure concerning powers of representation in your jurisdiction?
There is currently no publicly available guidance produced by the government on the law and procedure concerning powers of representation in the Cayman Islands.

Notes

1 Unreported FSD 199 of 2015 (IKJ) 19 January 2018.
2 [2004] EWCA Civ 1554.
3 (1870) LR 5 QB 549.

At the date of publication there is active consultancy with respect to the statutory introduction of enduring power of attorney and ancillary matters in the Cayman Islands. This chapter represents the law as at October 2024, and readers are accordingly encouraged to monitor developments.

China

Jason Tian
Shanghai Landing Law Offices

1. Does your jurisdiction have legislation providing for powers of representation such as ordinary, continuing, enduring or lasting powers of attorney?

Under China law, there is legislation for general powers of attorney which is used widely in civil and commercial settings with a specific purpose. However, there is no legislation for enduring or lasting powers of attorney that is used specifically for the purpose of taking care of the finances and medical matters of incapacitated persons.

However, China law has the 'consensual guardianship' law where an adult can enter into an agreement designating a person from his or her close family, or others willing to serve as guardians, to be his or her guardian in case he or she totally or partially loses mental capacity. In practice, in addition to and incidental to this agreement, a power of attorney will be designed and signed by the designator to allow the appointed guardian to act and deal with third parties. This power of attorney is in nature very similar to a lasting power of attorney.

It should be noted that in practice the concept of consensual guardianship has not developed to its full extent, much has yet to be clarified and tested in practice. The appointed guardian, even with a notarised power of representation, may well encounter difficulty when dealing with third parties on their behalf.

There are no clear rules for determining mental capacity. A person of 18 years old will be assumed to have mental capacity. The China Civil Procedures Law has prescribed a special proceeding for determining and declaring a person's mental capacity if it is in doubt.

2. When do powers of representation come into effect?
For a general power of attorney, it takes effect upon execution by the principal. There are no specific formalities on how a power of attorney shall be executed in order to be valid but, in practice, in the case of consensual guardianship, the execution of a power of attorney is generally notarised to make the power of attorney more formal.

3. Does your jurisdiction have a legal test for determining mental capacity?
There are no clear rules for determining mental capacity. A person of 18 years old will be assumed to have mental capacity. The China Civil Procedures Law has prescribed a special proceeding for determining and declaring a person's mental capacity if it is in doubt. In obvious cases, there is no need for forensic assessment of mental capacity and the judges may directly decide on the issue. When necessary, the court will refer to a forensic assessment in order to make the decision.

4. Can the powers of representation deal with property and finances and/or health and welfare?
China law is not clear on this but, in practice, the power of attorney could be used to deal with both finances and health and medical issues. It would be advisable to list the desired powers in the power of attorney so there is no doubt as to instructions.

5. Are there any other protective measures available?
As the law of 'consensual guardianship' is relatively new, no implementation rules have been promulgated so far. Also, there are not any rules concerning the oversight of the performance of duties by the designated guardians/attorneys.

6. What are the formalities of establishing a power of representation?
As there are no specific rules about the set-up and enforcement of consensual guardianship, an agreement between the designator and the designated guardian is required, and there are no legal formalities establishing such a power of attorney. In practice, to make it formal and strong in validity, the agreement and power of attorney in relation to the consensual guardianship are always notarised with a notary office in China.

7. Is there a registration process for powers of representation?
There is no registration process for a power of attorney in China. The power of attorney can be used as soon as it has been executed. But in the case of power of attorney for incapacitated persons or minor persons (where a guardian is appointed in a will by the minor's parents), it is advisable to resort to court proceedings to confirm the guardianship by court so as to pave the way for the guardians to act on behalf of the wards with third parties.

8. How can a power of representation be revoked or terminated (ie, in the event of marriage, divorce or death)?
There are no statutory provisions regarding revocation or termination of powers of attorney. The general rules for revocation or termination of a power of attorney would apply, for example, in the event of the death of the attorney which is a statutory cause of terminating a power of attorney.

The China Supreme Court has made it clear in its interpretations related to consensual guardianship that: (i) before the guardian-designating individual entirely or partially loses his or her mental capacity, either party may terminate the guardianship agreement; (ii) after the said individual entirely or partially loses his or her mental capacity, the appointed guardian may not terminate the guardianship agreement subject to court scrutiny; and (iii) if the attorney conducts his or her duties in a way which is harmful and detrimental to the legitimate interests of the ward then third parties as defined in Article 36 of the China Civil Code may apply to the court to terminate the guardianship.

9. Is the process of making and/or registering a power of representation supervised by a court or government body?
There is no such mechanism in place.

10. Is there a governmental or administrative body with oversight of the validity of a power of representation and supervision of its use?
There is no such mechanism in place.

11. What role do the courts in your jurisdiction have in relation to powers of representation?
China courts don't have an active role in overseeing the conclusion and enforcement of powers of representation, except for the limited roles described above. In reality, guardians may function much better with a court judgment/decision confirming his or her guardianship.

12. Are foreign powers of representation legally recognised in your jurisdiction? If so, what is the applicable legal framework?
There is no legislation in China regarding recognition of such foreign powers of representation. I am not aware of any precedent cases involving such foreign power of representation. However, there could be a chance that a power of representation duly signed under foreign laws might be recognised in China. These circumstances would be limited, such as collecting rent on behalf of the ward, provided that there is no foreign court sanctioning the validity of such powers of representation.

13. Has your jurisdiction ratified The Hague Convention on the International Protection of Adults 2000? If not, are there any plans for your jurisdiction to do so in the near future?
No, I am not aware of any imminent plans for China to ratify The Hague Convention.

14. Is there any publicly available guidance on the law and procedure concerning powers of representation in your jurisdiction?
I am not aware of such publicly available resources.

England and Wales

Kelly Greig
Blick Rothenberg

1. Does your jurisdiction have legislation providing for powers of representation such as ordinary, continuing, enduring or lasting powers of attorney?

Currently, in England and Wales, there are various types of power of attorney (POA) that could be in existence or could be put into existence:

- Power for a specific purpose – Donors may appoint persons to act on their behalf (attorneys) while they retain mental capacity but perhaps are not geographically available to deal with issues, for example, to sell a house or to obtain a grant of representation in respect of a deceased's estate. The specific purpose POA is limited to that specific purpose and remains in force until revoked by the donor; the purpose is completed or ceases to exist, or the donor loses mental capacity – such POA cannot be used for health and welfare decisions. This POA does not need to be registered.
- General POA – Donors may appoint attorneys to act in relation to all property and affair decisions under a blanket general POA.[1] This confers authority on the attorney to do on behalf of the donor anything that he or she could have lawfully done. Such POAs do not take any decision-making power away from the donor should he or she wish to make a specific decision. The power comes to an end should it be revoked by the donor, or he

or she loses mental capacity. This power does not need to be registered.

- Enduring power of attorney (EPA) – It has not been possible to make an EPA in England and Wales since October 2007, although those that made valid EPAs before that can still use them. The EPA can be used immediately by the attorney and relates to all property and financial decisions.

  If the attorney has reason to believe that the donor has become or is becoming mentally incapable of managing his or her affairs, the attorney must then apply for registration of the EPA. Such application is made to the Office of the Public Guardian and notifications must be made to at least three eligible family members based on set categories.

Registration can be challenged on a number of grounds.[2]

- Since October 2007, it is possible to make a lasting power of attorney (LPA). There are two different types: one for property and financial affairs (PFA) and one for health and welfare decisions (HW). There is no requirement for immediate registration, but they must be registered before they can be used, therefore commonly the recommendation is that they are registered straight away, such that they can be used as soon as needed.

  LPAs for PFA can be used while a donor retains capacity at his or her direction and then also when a donor loses capacity.

  LPAs for HW can only be used once the donor loses capacity.

  If a donor loses capacity and the LPA is not yet registered, the attorneys have an obligation to register it straight away.

  An LPA must be signed by a certificate provider who is either a professional in certain fields or someone who has known the donor for more than two years. Such certificate confirms that in the certificate provider's opinion the donor has sufficient mental capacity to make the POA and is not under any undue pressure to enter into the document.
- There is also provision for a trustee to delegate his or her authority by POA for a maximum period of 12 months.[3]

2. When do powers of representation come into effect?

- Powers for a specific purpose – upon the donor executing the POA document.
- General power of attorney – upon the donor executing the POA document.
- EPA – upon the donor executing the document and all the attorneys validly signing the document. If the donor loses or is losing capacity, the attorney must register the EPA to continue to use it.
- LPA PFA – upon valid registration of the document with the Office of the Public Guardian (OPG).

- LPA HW – upon valid registration of the document with the OPG and the donor lacking the required mental capacity to make the specific decision in question.

For both the LPA and EPA, the donor can insert a clause specifying that the document is not to be used until the donor loses capacity, usually with the requirement that a particular type of doctor certifies that the donor is not able to manage his or her affairs.

3. Does your jurisdiction have a legal test for determining mental capacity?

Mental capacity in England and Wales is decision-specific and there is a presumption that a person has capacity unless it is established that he or she lacks capacity,[4] and case law and legislation are both in place setting out the correct test of mental capacity for each decision that is made, for example:

- making a will – *Banks v Goodfellow*[5]
- making a gift – *Re Beaney*[6]
- to marry – *Sheffield City Council v E*[7]
- to make an LPA – *The Public Guardian v RI & Ors*[8]

The Mental Capacity Act 2005 (MCA) is probably the biggest piece of legislation that we have governing issues of mental capacity. This sets out the inherent jurisdiction of the court to make decisions on behalf of those who lack capacity, including the appointment of deputies on behalf of the court should someone lacking capacity not have a valid LPA or EPA[9] subject to the requirement that any decision should be in the best interests of the donor.[10]

4. Can the power of representation deal with property and finances and/or health and welfare?

The specific power, general power, EPA and LPA (PFA) all deal with property and finances with only the EPA and LPA (PFA) being able to be used after the loss of mental capacity.

It is only the LPA (HW) that can be used for health and welfare decisions and that is only if the individual has lost the necessary mental capacity to make that decision. The LPA (HW) allows attorneys to make decisions about life-sustaining treatment of the donor but only if the donor has selected this option.

5. Are there any other protective measures available?

For those who lack capacity and do not have a valid LPA or EPA (perhaps because they never made one or the power has been revoked), the Court of Protection (COP) has authority under the MCA to make specific decisions on behalf of the individual.[11]

In addition, where it is likely that it will be necessary to make a series of decisions on behalf of an individual who lacks capacity on an ongoing basis, the court may delegate this function to an individual or trust corporation – that person is known as a deputy and has power to manage the general affairs of an individual subject to any limitations in the order.[12]

There are also restrictions on a deputy's authority[13] and some matters are still reserved for the court, for example, making a will on behalf of that person, or gifting significant sums when it comes to health and personal welfare decisions, the COP prefers generally not to delegate those decisions, such that each one must be brought specifically to the court. However, in certain circumstances, where there are a large number of personal welfare decisions that need to be made for an individual and the potential deputy has proved capable, the court may appoint a personal welfare deputy for such decisions.

In the absence of an LPA (HW) or a personal welfare deputy, there are a number of everyday decisions relating to, for example, food, clothing or general medication that can be made under the 'best interests' criteria.[14]

6. What are the formalities of establishing a power of representation?

For all powers, the donor must have the requisite mental capacity to enter into the document. Notably:

- a specific power is generally done by deed and witnessed;
- a general power is signed as a deed and witnessed;
- an EPA is signed as a deed and witnessed, the attorneys also having to sign, and their signature witnessed; and
- an LPA is signed as a deed and witnessed, signed by a certificate provider and the attorneys also having to sign and their signature witnessed.

7. Is there a registration process of representation?

	Yes	No
Specific powers		✓
General powers		✓
EPA	✓*	
LPA	✓**	

* There is a registration process once the donor starts to lose mental capacity; this requires notification of certain family members who have an opportunity to object. The attorney(s) register the EPA.
** There is a registration process which must be undertaken before the document is used. The process involves the OPG notifying anyone the donor may have asked to be notified in the document. This gives individuals a chance to object to registration within a specific time. The donor or the attorney(s) can register the LPA.

8. How can a power of representation be revoked or terminated (ie, in the event of marriage, divorce or death)?

No POA can continue after the death of the donor as at that time the attorney's powers cease.

If the attorney is the spouse or civil partner of the donor, the attorney's appointment automatically ends if they divorce or get an annulment unless the donor had stated in the document that the attorney can continue to act after these events.

The donor can revoke any type of power while they retain the necessary capacity to do so. Such revocation is usually undertaken by a deed of revocation and, in respect of registered powers, the deed must be sent to the OPG such that the powers can be cancelled.

Specific and general powers terminate once the donor has lost the necessary mental capacity to manage his or her property and affairs, and in respect of the specific purpose POA, once the deputy has lost capacity to undertake that specific purpose.

The attorneys can choose to disclaim their appointment at any point.[15]

In relation to an LPA if it has already been registered, the donor must also notify the OPG (form LPA0005) and return any copies they have of the LPA to the OPG.

If there is more than one attorney and the power is joint and several, the remaining attorney may continue to act. If there is no remaining attorney to act or the power is only to be used on a joint basis, then either the donor must make a new LPA or if they have already lost capacity, an application for a deputy to be appointed.

Attorneys can also be removed if they become bankrupt or if the court determines that they are not discharging their duties appropriately, for example, in cases of financial abuse and wilful neglect.

9. Is the process of making and/or registering a power of representation supervised by a court or government body?

The process of making a POA is not supervised in any way. However, for those documents that require registration (EPAs and LPAs), the OPG deals with the registration of those documents.

10. Is there a governmental or administrative body with oversight of the validity of a power of representation and supervision of its use?

Applications for registration of EPAs and LPAs are made to the OPG which reviews the documents to ensure proper execution and in cases of doubt (clauses that are not allowed, objections received for registration etc) they will refer the matter to the Court of Protection for the court to consider the relevant submission.

The day-to-day supervision of the attorneys under registered EPAs or LPAs is carried out by the OPG. This is a fairly light touch in comparison to the deputy regime which requires annual reports and a bond lodged.

Complaints about an attorney's actions are made to the OPG which will investigate and if it is felt there is a case for removal of an attorney, it will bring proceedings against the attorney in the COP, where ultimately the court will make a decision.

The OPG does not supervise attorneys under a specific or general power. Complaints about abuse of power would need to be taken to the court.

11. What role do the courts in your jurisdiction have in relation to powers of representation?

The COP gets involved where there are issues as to validity of execution of the power, challenges of duress, undue influence and a lack of capacity when signing as well as severance of certain powers the donor may have inserted into the LPA which are not compatible with the document or not allowed. In addition, the attorney can be removed if the court considers there is sufficient cause. Direct applications can be made to the court in this respect.

Finally, the court will become involved if any application is made to it by the attorney for permission to undertake an action which is currently in excess of the attorney's powers.

12. Are foreign powers of representation legally recognised in your jurisdiction? If so, what is the applicable framework?
Under the MCA, a protective measure taken in relation to an adult under the law of a country other than England and Wales is generally to be recognised if it was taken on the ground that the adult is habitually resident in the other country[16] and therefore can be enforced in England and Wales.[17]

Generally, foreign POAs are not usually protective measures as these require some degree of intervention by a foreign state[18] although the situation may be different if there is state intervention in the form of confirmation or registration.

However, the court can make a declaration that an attorney under a foreign power is acting lawfully when acting in England and Wales.[19]

13. Has your jurisdiction ratified The Hague Convention on the International Protection of Adults 2000? If not, are there any plans for your jurisdiction to do so in the near future?
The United Kingdom was a signatory to the convention but has only ratified it in respect of Scotland. Therefore, England and Wales have not ratified and there are no immediate plans for the United Kingdom to ratify this on behalf of England and Wales in the near future.

However, the MCA gives effect to the convention and makes related provision as to the private international law of England and Wales.[20]

An Article 38 certificate given by an authority in a convention country is to be accepted, unless there is contrary evidence that the information contained is incorrect.[21]

However, crucially because the convention is not itself in force, the existence of a foreign power of attorney does not prevent the Court of Protection from exercising its best interests jurisdiction[22] under Sections 15 and 16 of the MCA 2005.

In practice, no institution will accept a foreign POA without an order from the COP confirming its enforceability in England and Wales.

14. Is there any publicly available guidance on the law and procedure concerning powers of representation in your jurisdiction?
The OPG website which is within the UK government website contains

lots of useful information on LPAs, including the making, regulation, process and removal of attorneys. In addition, there are also helpful guides on duties and obligations of an attorney as well as the limitation of the attorney's powers.

In terms of specific and general powers other than the primary legislation and case law, such guidance is limited to articles on law firm websites.

Notes

1 Also known as a Section 10 POA – as it is referred to in the Power of Attorney Act 1971.
2 Enduring Powers of Attorney Act 1985, Section 6(5).
3 Trustee Act 1925, Section 69(2) – further discussion around this POA is beyond the scope of this Special Report.
4 Mental Capacity Act 2005 (MCA), Section 1.
5 (1870) LR 5 QB 549.
6 [1978] 1 WLR 770.
7 [2004] EWHC 2808 (Fam).
8 [2022] EWCOP 22.
9 MCA, Section 16.
10 MCA, Section 4.
11 MCA, Section 16(2)(a).
12 MCA, Section 16(2)(b).
13 MCA, Section 20.
14 MCA, Section 4.
15 Form LPA0005 must be completed for LPAs and the original sent to the donor and copies sent to all other attorneys.
16 MCA, Section 19 and Schedule 3.
17 MCA, Section 22 and Court of Protection Rules 2017 (COPR), Rule 23.4.
18 *Re Various Applications Concerning Foreign Representative Powers* [2019] EWCOP 52.
19 MCA, Section 15 and COPR, Rule 23.6.
20 MCA, Part 3, Section 63 and Schedule 3.
21 MCA, Section 30 and Schedule 3.
22 *Re Various Applications Concerning Foreign Representative Powers* [2019] EWCOP 52.

Guernsey

Sandra Duerden
Gilly Kennedy-Smith
William Ostick
Mourant

1. Does your jurisdiction have legislation providing for powers of representation such as ordinary, continuing, enduring or lasting powers of attorney?

The States of Guernsey have introduced the Capacity (Bailiwick of Guernsey) Law 2020 (the Law) and the Capacity (Lasting Powers of Attorney) (Bailiwick of Guernsey) Ordinance 2022 (the Ordinance). The Ordinance came into effect on 1 April 2022 and permits persons to create lasting powers of attorney (LPAs). The Electronic Transactions (Guernsey) Law 2000 provides that powers of attorney for individuals must be executed in wet ink, not electronically.

Ordinary powers of attorney executed by individuals can also be prepared. They must be executed in accordance with the Powers of Attorney and Affidavit (Bailiwick of Guernsey) Law 1995, usually before a notary public. If intended for use abroad they may need to be apostilled.

Powers of attorney provided by Guernsey companies generally do not need to be executed before notaries and must comply with the Companies (Guernsey) Law 2008 (as amended). If intended for foreign use, they may need to be apostilled.

Powers of attorney provided by trustees must comply with the Trusts (Guernsey) Law 2007 (as amended). Unless the terms of the trust

A key principle of the Capacity (Bailiwick of Guernsey) Law 2020 is the presumption of capacity. It should be assumed that the person has the capacity to make his or her own decisions, unless it can be established that he or she lacks capacity.

provide to the contrary, they may only be granted for a maximum of three years.

2. When do powers of representation come into effect?

A health and welfare LPA can only be used when the grantor has lost capacity to make relevant decisions and must be activated before the attorney can act. In the case of a property and financial affairs LPA, the grantor has a choice for the LPA to be either immediately effective or effective upon a loss of capacity. An LPA can only be relied upon once activated.

3. Does your jurisdiction have a legal test for determining mental capacity?

Yes, the Law provides a modern legal framework to support and protect people who lack capacity to make decisions for themselves, and to allow others to act on their behalf in their best interests.

A key principle of the Law is the presumption of capacity. It should be assumed that the person has the capacity to make his or her own decisions, unless it can be established that he or she lacks capacity.

To determine whether someone has capacity to make a specific decision, the Law provides a two-stage test. This requires consideration of whether:

- the decision maker is able to make the decision (the functional assessment); and
- if the decision maker is unable to do so, whether this inability is due to an impairment of, or a disturbance of the functioning of the mind or the brain, whether permanent or temporary (the diagnostic assessment).

A capacity assessment should show, on the balance of probabilities, that the person in question lacks capacity to make the specific decision. The person completing the capacity assessment should demonstrate that he or she has a 'reasonable belief' that an individual lacks capacity to make the relevant decision. There are a number of reasons why someone might question another's capacity to make a specific decision. These include:

- behaviour or circumstances which suggest that a connected person has doubts about the decision maker's capacity to make his or her own decision;
- a situation where the decision maker demonstrates the inability to make a specific decision;
- someone who knows the decision maker raises concern about his or her capacity;

- the decision maker's planning is not planning that the person expects to see; and
- the decision maker has been diagnosed with a mental disorder and has already been assessed as lacking capacity to make other decisions.

Generally, under the Law a capacity assessment to determine whether the decision maker has capacity to make a particular decision does not need to be completed by a person who is professionally qualified but the more onerous or significant the decision, the more likely it is that professionals will be relied upon in the capacity assessment. The person who assesses an individual's capacity to make a particular decision will usually be the person who is involved in that decision. For example, the doctor proposing treatment, the advocate arranging for a will to be signed or a carer to determine if someone needs to take medication. In practice, many determinations as to capacity will require additional support or consultation.

4. Can the powers of representation deal with property and finances and/or health and welfare?

Yes, both types of LPA are available in Guernsey. They can be completed as combined or separate LPAs.

5. Are there any other protective measures available?

Where an individual is unable to manage his or her own affairs due to a lack of capacity or some form of infirmity and has not made an LPA, or by virtue of being a minor, it is necessary for a person or persons to be appointed as a guardian by the court to manage that individual's affairs. This may be due to an individual no longer being mentally capable or due to illness. The guardian is often a close relative but can also be a friend or professional person. More than one guardian can be appointed, if required.

An application to the court must be made, supported by a family council. This is normally made up of the closest blood relatives to the applicant. The family council will be required to attend court with the applicant if they are able to.

A medical opinion will also need to be provided by a medical professional in the form of an affidavit. The doctor swearing the affidavit must have seen the patient in question not more than six weeks prior to the court hearing.

The appointment of a guardian does not give the guardian power to sell the individual's realty (houses and land). For the guardian to do so, it is necessary to make a further application to the court seeking permission to sell the individual's realty.

6. What are the formalities of establishing a power of representation?

An LPA can only be made if the grantor has capacity to understand the LPA form and its contents and effect. The prescribed LPA form must be completed and signed by the grantor and attorneys in the presence of witnesses. A witness cannot be one of the grantor's attorneys. It is not necessary for the grantor and attorneys to sign at the same time. However, the grantor must sign the form before it is signed by the attorneys.

The completed form must be registered at HM Greffier which is the Official Clerk of the Royal Court in Guernsey. The grantor will need to attend in person, with proof of identity (photo ID and birth certificate) and to have paid the relevant fee. The grantor will be requested to confirm his or her wish that HM Greffier will register the LPA and, provided there are no issues, it will be promptly registered.

As stated at question 2 above, the LPA for property and financial affairs can be used, with the grantor's permission, before a loss of capacity if this has been elected within the form, otherwise it can only be used once the grantor has lost capacity and once the LPA has been activated. The LPA for health and welfare can only be used if the grantor has lost capacity and once the LPA has been activated.

A separate form is available for activation of the LPA. The attorney must request a capacity assessment to establish whether the grantor has lost capacity. The capacity assessment can be completed by the grantor's GP, consultant or other health or social care professional. Those people are referred to as 'prescribed persons' under the Ordinance, and are listed at Part II, Section 4 of the Capacity (Lasting Powers of Attorney) (Miscellaneous) Regulations 2022. The professional who completes the capacity assessment will complete the certificate to state that the grantor does not have capacity to make the relevant decision and therefore the LPA can be activated.

If HM Greffier is satisfied that the grantor has been assessed to lack capacity, such that the LPA can be activated, the Register of Lasting Powers of Attorney will be updated and the LPA will be activated. The activation certificate should be kept with the LPA. The attorney will be able to make relevant decisions in accordance with the LPA once this has been activated.

If HM Greffier believes that the grantor still has capacity or is concerned about the circumstances of the capacity assessment, the LPA will not be activated and the attorney cannot make decisions for the grantor. The grantor or the attorney may appeal against the decision of HM Greffier in the Royal Court.

7. Is there a registration process for powers of representation?
Yes, see question 6 above.

8. How can a power of representation be revoked or terminated (ie, in the event of marriage, divorce or death)?
A grantor can cancel an LPA at any time, provided he or she has the capacity to do so. It does not matter if the LPA has been activated or not. This can only be done by attending HM Greffier in person.

If a grantor names his or her spouse or civil partner as attorney and they later get divorced or lawfully separated, this will end the spouse or civil partner's appointment unless specifically stated otherwise in the LPA. If a grantor names his or her spouse or civil partner as one of only two attorneys and they are to act jointly, divorce or lawful separation will also revoke the LPA. Marriage would not automatically revoke an LPA but it should be viewed as an opportunity to review the LPA and, if the grantor has capacity, consideration given to expressly revoking it by attending HM Greffier and replacing it.

An LPA will expire upon death. It is worth noting that an LPA cannot be used to change the will of the grantor.

9. Is the process of making and/or registering a power of representation supervised by a court or government body?
Yes, registration and activation must be approved by HM Greffier.

10. Is there a governmental or administrative body with oversight of the validity of a power of representation and supervision of its use?
Questions or issues as to the validity and use of LPAs in Guernsey are decided by HM Greffier.

The Committee for Health and Social Care safeguards the rights of people who lack capacity, as well as promoting opportunities for those people to make their own decisions. It is committed to ensuring the highest professional standards are demonstrated by all those involved when the Law is being used, so far as it is able.

The committee updates its policies and practices, provides practical training, publishes a Code of Practice on capacity and works with stakeholders to ensure that the Law is implemented across the Bailiwick in a consistent and practical manner. The committee is not, however, a regulator of specific registered LPAs.

11. What role do the courts in your jurisdiction have in relation to powers of representation?
HM Greffier is responsible for overseeing the registration, activation

and revocation of LPAs in Guernsey. It also manages the Register of Lasting Powers of Attorney, which is updated every time there are changes to the status of registered LPAs. Decisions made by HM Greffier in relation to LPAs may be appealed in the Royal Court. In addition, if joint attorneys under an LPA are unable to reach agreement in respect of a particular decision, then that decision can only be made by an application to the Royal Court.

12. Are foreign powers of representation legally recognised in your jurisdiction? If so, what is the applicable legal framework?
It is possible to register certain foreign enduring and lasting powers of attorney in Guernsey. The Royal Court has an established process for the registration of LPAs which have been made in the United Kingdom. The registration of LPAs from other jurisdictions may be more difficult, depending on the formalities and processes required in that foreign jurisdiction.

The process requires an application to the Royal Court. It is usually done where a non-Guernsey resident has movable assets located in Guernsey, such as a bank account or investment portfolio. It is always preferable to have a Guernsey LPA for Guernsey assets, however, in-person meetings at HM Greffier are not always possible for all clients. Local home and hospital visits can be arranged at the point of registration.

13. Has your jurisdiction ratified The Hague Convention on the International Protection of Adults 2000? If not, are there any plans for your jurisdiction to do so in the near future?
The United Kingdom has ratified The Hague Convention on the International Protection of Adults 2000 but at this time it does not extend to any Crown Dependencies.

The United Kingdom is responsible for representing Guernsey (and the wider Bailiwick) internationally, which includes international agreements. The longstanding practice of the United Kingdom when it ratifies, accedes to or accepts an international agreement is to do so on behalf of the United Kingdom of Great Britain and Northern Ireland and any of the Crown Dependencies (which includes the Bailiwick of Guernsey, comprising the separate jurisdictions of Guernsey, Alderney and Sark) or Overseas Territories that wish the agreement to apply to them.

The United Kingdom's ratification, accession or acceptance can also be extended at a later date. This means that, when the United Kingdom is planning to ratify a particular international agreement, it should consult the Crown Dependencies about whether they wish to have it extended to them (which aligns with Guernsey's 2008

International Identity Framework). The Crown Dependencies are generally not automatically included in the United Kingdom's ratification of, accession to or acceptance of a treaty unless expressly listed.

14. Is there any publicly available guidance on the law and procedure concerning powers of representation in your jurisdiction?

Yes, the Committee for Health and Social Care has released a Code of Practice, intended to give clear and accessible guidance to practitioners and others performing duties and exercising powers under the Law. The Royal Court has also issued guidance for how to create an LPA. Both are available from the States of Guernsey and Royal Court of Guernsey websites, respectively. HM Greffier has also published forms and guidance.

Hong Kong

Sherlynn G Chan
Deacons

1. Does your jurisdiction have legislation providing for powers of representation such as ordinary, continuing, enduring or lasting powers of attorney?

Yes, Hong Kong currently has two specific laws providing for powers of representation, namely the Powers of Attorney Ordinance (Cap 31) and the Enduring Powers of Attorney Ordinance (Cap 501).

The Powers of Attorney Ordinance governs the creation and execution of a general power of attorney (POA) and outlines the essential requirements for creating a valid POA in Hong Kong including the specific form and content of the instrument and the execution procedures as a deed.

The Enduring Powers of Attorney Ordinance allows for an enduring power of attorney (EPA) to be executed while the donor is mentally capable which continues to have effect after the donor becomes mentally incapable, contrary to a conventional/general POA which becomes invalid when the donor becomes mentally incapacitated.

2. When do powers of representation come into effect?

Generally speaking, the POA comes into effect upon execution and the EPA's commencement will depend on its terms, which can come into effect at the time of execution or upon the date or event specified in the EPA.

3. Does your jurisdiction have a legal test for determining mental capacity?

In Hong Kong, there is no specific legislation for determining mental capacity and the legal tests for determining mental capacity under different ordinances vary. Generally speaking, mental capacity refers to the mental competence and decision-making ability of an individual. Pursuant to common law, mental capacity is presumed and the determination of mental capacity is decision-specific and time-specific.

The mental capacity required to make a valid will (ie, testamentary capacity) derives from common law. The four criteria for testamentary capacity in the classic statement by Cockburn CJ[1] have been endorsed in a number of Hong Kong cases,[2] namely that a testator must:

- understand the nature of the act and its effects;
- understand the extent of the property of which he or she is disposing;
- be able to comprehend and appreciate the claims to which he or she ought to give effect; and
- be free from disorder of mind or delusion that would poison his or her affections, pervert his or her sense of right, or prevent the exercise of his or her natural faculties.

The Enduring Powers of Attorney Ordinance defines 'mentally incapable' and 'mental incapacity' by reference to Section 1A of the Powers of Attorney Ordinance, ie, a person is regarded as being mentally incapable, if:

- he or she is suffering from a mental disorder or mental handicap and (i) is unable to understand the effect of the power of attorney; or (ii) is unable by reason of his or her mental disorder or mental handicap to make a decision to grant a power of attorney; or
- he or she is unable to communicate to any other person who has made a reasonable effort to understand him or her, any intention or wish to grant a power of attorney.

Under Part II of the Mental Health Ordinance (Cap 136), if a person is certified by two medical doctors (one of whom has to be an approved doctor) to be mentally incapable of managing and administering his property and affairs, the court has the power to appoint a committee with specific authority to manage his property and affairs (Part II Committee). The statutory definition of whether a person is mentally incapacitated under the Mental Health Ordinance is, however, different from that of an EPA or a POA as discussed above.

Under Section 2(1) of the Mental Health Ordinance, 'mental incapacity' is construed to mean 'mental disorder' or 'mental handicap'. In particular, for the purposes of the appointment of a committee under Part II of the Mental Health Ordinance, a 'mentally incapacitated person' means a person who is incapable, by reason of mental incapacity, of managing and administering his or her property and affairs.

For other purposes under the Mental Health Ordinance, such as an application for guardianship under Part IVB, a 'mentally incapacitated person' is construed to mean a 'patient' or a 'mentally handicapped person' as defined in the said ordinance.

4. Can the powers of representation deal with property and finances and/or health and welfare?

In Hong Kong, both the POA and EPA can deal with property and finances of the donor. However, there is currently no legislation which allows appointment of a representative to specifically deal with the donor's health and welfare matters.

Due to the limitations of EPAs, the Department of Justice proposed a Continuing Power of Attorney Bill for a new Continuing Powers of Attorney (CPA) regime in December 2017. It will replace the existing EPA regime in Hong Kong when enacted, but EPAs executed prior to that would continue to be governed by the Enduring Powers of Attorney Ordinance.

The new regime extends CPAs to cover directions in relation to the donor's personal care as well as financial matters. A CPA, similar to an EPA, also survives the subsequent mental incapacity of the donor. There are also requirements relating to the use of a prescribed form as the instrument to create a CPA based on those in Section 3(1) and (2) of the Enduring Powers of Attorney Ordinance.

The timeline for enacting the legislation remains uncertain as the government indicated that further time is required to address issues such as the practical implementation of a CPA alongside an advance directive, as well as determining the individuals authorised to access the register of CPAs.[3]

5. Are there any other protective measures available?

Pursuant to Section 18(3) of the Enduring Powers of Attorney Ordinance and Section 6 of the Enduring Powers of Attorney (Prescribed Form) Regulation (Cap 501A), the donor may nominate persons to be notified when the attorney applies for the registration of the EPA with the High Court Registry, failing which the court may draw an adverse inference in any legal proceedings relating to the EPA.

Section 11 of the Enduring Powers of Attorney Ordinance provides for an effective mechanism to protect the donor, ie, the court may upon the application of an interested party:

- require the attorney to produce records and accounts and make an order for their auditing;
- revoke or vary the enduring power; or
- remove the attorney if satisfied that the interests of the donor of an enduring power so require it.

In Hong Kong, the Mental Health Court's jurisdiction comes into play when protective measures have to be made for a mentally incapacitated person, in particular where consensus cannot be reached among the family members and carers of the mentally incapacitated person. The paramount consideration of the Mental Health Court is always the best interests of the mentally incapacitated person. In the context of an appointment of a Part II Committee, the Mental Health Court has a wide range of powers to do or secure the doing of things that are necessary or expedient for maintaining and administering the property and affairs of the mentally incapacitated person.

Section 59J of the Mental Health Ordinance further establishes the Guardianship Board, a legal quasi-judicial tribunal which conducts hearings to make guardianship orders for mentally incapacitated persons who have attained the age of 18 years. The Guardianship Board attaches significant importance to protecting the interests of a mentally incapacitated person who is subject to a guardianship order (the Subject) when exercising its powers in the appointment of a guardian. Where it appears that there is no appropriate person available to be appointed as guardian of the Subject, the Guardianship Board will appoint the Director of Social Welfare as the public guardian of the Subject.[4]

Section 59U provides for a review of the guardianship order. Thus, in the event of any suspected abuse of power, change in circumstances or concerns that the guardian is not promoting the interests of the Subject, an application for review can be made.

In the performance of any functions or exercise of any powers, the guardian shall ensure that the interests of the Subject are promoted, and in so far as the views and wishes of the Subject may be ascertained, such views and wishes should be respected.[5]

6. What are the formalities of establishing a power of representation?

Under the Powers of Attorney Ordinance, an instrument creating a POA must be executed by deed. Pursuant to Section 7 of the Powers of Attorney Ordinance, a general POA can be made in the statutory form set out in the schedule thereto.

Under the Enduring Powers of Attorney Ordinance, an EPA must be made in prescribed forms: Form 1 for appointment of one attorney, and Form 2 for more than one attorney. Pursuant to Section 5 of the said ordinance, the EPA must also be signed in the presence of a Hong Kong registered solicitor and Hong Kong registered medical practitioner, and countersigned by the attorney(s).

7. Is there a registration process for powers of representation?

Section 9 of the Enduring Powers of Attorney Ordinance requires the registration of an EPA at the High Court Registry when the attorney has reason to believe that the donor is or is becoming mentally incapable.

The registration process includes submitting the original and a certified copy of the EPA to the High Court Registry together with copies of the practising certificates of both the solicitor and the registered medical practitioner who witnessed the execution of the EPA at the relevant time, and payment of the prescribed fees.

8. How can a power of representation be revoked or terminated (ie, in the event of marriage, divorce or death)?

Generally speaking, a POA or an EPA can be terminated at the donor's instruction. Under common law, a POA can also be revoked by lapse of time (in the case of a POA granted for a limited period); or by the death, incapacity or bankruptcy of the donor.

Section 13 of the Enduring Powers of Attorney Ordinance further stipulates the circumstances under which an EPA is revoked, namely:

- if the donor revokes it when he or she is mentally capable, or if after the registration, the donor revokes it after his or her recovery;
- on the bankruptcy of the attorney;
- if a court makes an order for its revocation under Section 11(1)(b) or for the removal of an attorney under Section 11(1)(c);
- on the appointment of a committee pursuant to Part II of the Mental Health Ordinance, if the court gives a direction revoking the enduring power;
- on the death of the donor or the attorney; or
- subject to the ordinance, on any ground on which a power of attorney is revoked at common law.

9. Is the process of making and/or registering a power of representation supervised by a court or government body?
The making of a POA or EPA is not supervised by a court or government body. Under the Enduring Powers of Attorney Ordinance, the registration of an EPA must be made with the High Court Registry and the Registrar of the High Court shall register an EPA if satisfied that all the requisite requirements relating to the creation and registration of an EPA have been complied with.[6]

However, it should be noted that the registrar will not inquire into or determine the validity of the EPA upon registration. The registration of an invalidly executed EPA will not validate the same.[7]

10. Is there a governmental or administrative body with oversight of the validity of a power of representation and supervision of its use?
No, there is currently no government or administrative body in Hong Kong with oversight of the validity and supervision of the use of a power of representation. However, a challenge to the validity of a power of representation or the improper use thereof may be made with the Hong Kong courts.

11. What role do the courts in your jurisdiction have in relation to powers of representation?
The Hong Kong courts have a supervisory role in determining the validity and proper use of the powers of representation.

12. Are foreign powers of representation legally recognised in your jurisdiction? If so, what is the applicable legal framework?
No.

13. Has your jurisdiction ratified The Hague Convention on the International Protection of Adults 2000? If not, are there any plans for your jurisdiction to do so in the near future?
No. It is unclear whether Hong Kong will ratify The Hague Convention on the International Protection of Adults 2000 in the near future.

14. Is there any publicly available guidance on the law and procedure concerning powers of representation in your jurisdiction?
There is currently no official publicly available guidance on the law and procedure concerning powers of representation. However, various articles have been written on the topic and there is a community legal information website called the "Community Legal Information Centre"[8] established and managed by the University of Hong Kong, which provides the public with legal information on various legal topics, including the relevant law and legal proceedings concerning powers of representation.

In 2018, Hong Kong University Press published a book entitled *A Practical Guide to Mental Health Law in Hong Kong*[9] which has a section on EPA.

The Department of Justice has also published an information leaflet entitled "Enduring Powers of Attorney – General Information"[10] in both Chinese and English for public reference.

Notes

1 See *Banks v Goodfellow* (1870) LR 5 QB 549 at 565.
2 See, eg, *Re Estate of Au Kong Tim* [2018] 2 HKLRD 864.
3 Hong Kong (China) Legislative Council (28 June 2023), *Official Record of Proceedings*, https://legco.primo.exlibrisgroup.com/discovery/delivery/852LEGCO_INST:LEGCO/1245855070006976.
4 Mental Health Ordinance, Section 59S(2).
5 *Ibid*, Section 59S(3).
6 Enduring Powers of Attorney Ordinance, Section 9(2).
7 *Ibid*, Section 9(7).
8 See https://clic.org.hk/en.
9 Sherlynn G Chan, *A Practical Guide to Mental Health Law in Hong Kong* (Hong Kong University Press, 2018).
10 See www.doj.gov.hk/en/archive/pdf/EPA_leaflet.pdf.

Ireland

Margaret Walsh
Sheil Solicitors LLP

1. Does your jurisdiction have legislation providing for powers of representation such as ordinary, continuing, enduring or lasting powers of attorney?

The law governing powers of attorney in Ireland was revised by the Powers of Attorney Act 1996 (the 1996 Act). This legislation which came into force on 1 August 1996,[1] overhauled the law relating to powers of attorney generally,[2] by making alterations to the common law rules, replacing the previous statutory provisions[3] governing such powers and introducing the concept of an enduring power of attorney,[4] to be regulated by the Office of Wards of Court.

Legislation amending the Powers of Attorney Act 1996, the Assisted Decision-Making (Capacity) Act 2015 (the 2015 Act)[5] and the Assisted Decision-Making (Capacity) (Amendment) Act 2022 (the 2022 Amendment Act) became operative on 26 April 2023[6] with regard to enduring powers of attorney and powers of representation generally.

Enduring powers of attorney made prior to 26 April 2023 continue to be governed by the 1996 Act. Enduring powers of attorney made after 25 April 2023 are governed by the Assisted Decision-Making (Capacity) Act 2015[7] and, in particular, by Part 7 of that act.

The Decision Support Service (DSS) was set up under the 2015 Act to promote the rights and interests of people who may need support with decision making.

2. When do powers of representation come into effect?

An enduring power of attorney (EPA) made on or after 26 April 2023 will take effect when each of the following three events have occurred:

- the EPA has been registered with the DSS;[8]
- the donor[9] becomes incapacitated and is unable to manage his or her affairs; and
- the DSS has been notified and is satisfied as to the donor's incapacity.

An EPA made prior to 26 April 2023 will take effect when registered with the Office of Wards of Court[10] on application by the attorney[11] to the registrar when the donor becomes, or is becoming, incapable of managing his or her affairs through loss of capacity as defined in the Powers of Attorney Act 1996 and established by medical evidence.[12]

3. Does your jurisdiction have a legal test for determining mental capacity?

A key feature of the 2015 Act is the introduction of a functional test for mental capacity.

The 2015 Act gives a very specific definition of what it means to lack capacity for the purposes of the act. It is a legal, not a medical, test and to apply the test the 2015 Act sets out how a relevant person's capacity is to be assessed and provides that a person lacks the capacity to make a decision if he or she is unable to:[13]

- understand information relevant to the decision;
- retain that information long enough to make a voluntary choice;
- use or weigh the information as part of the process of making the decision; or
- communicate his or her decision (whether by talking, writing, using sign language, assistive technology, or any other means) or, if the implementation of the decisions requires the act of a third party, to communicate by any means with that third party.

The assessment is accordingly based on the person's ability to make a decision. However, this assessment is both issue and time-specific, more particularly a person's capacity shall be assessed on the basis of his or her ability to understand the nature and consequence of a decision to be made by him or her in the context of the available choices at the time the decision is made.

4. Can the powers of representation deal with property and finances and/or health and welfare?

EPAs made under either the 1996 Act or 2015 Act can allow for decisions by the appointed attorney relating to property and affairs and/or personal welfare, unless the instrument creating the EPA limits the authority of the attorney to deal with the affairs of the donor. An EPA can grant general authority to the attorney in relation to all of the donor's property and affairs or may confine the authority to specific acts or decisions on the donor's behalf. Authority can also be given in relation to personal care decisions.

Decisions relating to future health (such as consent to or refusal of medical treatment) cannot be provided for in an EPA and are excluded for enduring powers of attorney under the 2015 Act.[14]

5. Are there any other protective measures available?

In addition to EPAs the 2015 Act provides for three arrangements to support persons over 18 with capacity issues in making decisions in relation to their property and their affairs. These arrangements are tiered in terms of the level of decision-making support or assistance needed by the relevant person,[15] also referred to as "the supported person".

5.1 Decision-making assistant

A decision-making assistant is appointed with the agreement of the supported person and can help the supported person with decisions specified in the decision-making assistance agreement. The decision-making assistant can help with accessing relevant information and records where this is included in the agreement and will have authority to gather and explain relevant information for the supported person and to help the supported person understand and weigh up any options or choices.

5.2 Co-decision-maker

A co-decision-maker is chosen by the supported person to assist and work with him or her in making specified joint decisions relating to personal care, property and/or financial matters.

5.3 Decision-making representative

The Circuit Court is given jurisdiction to appoint a decision-making representative to act on behalf of and make decisions for a person lacking capacity to manage his or her affairs (the supported person). Decisions that can be made by a court-appointed representative will be set out in the Decision-Making Representative Order made by the court and can include property and financial matters.

An enduring power of attorney must be in writing and include specific statements by the donor, the attorney, a medical practitioner and a legal practitioner, and must confirm the donor's capacity and understanding of the implications of creating the enduring power of attorney.

6. What are the formalities of establishing a power of representation?

The formalities will vary with the level of authority given by the power of representation.

An enduring power of attorney must be in writing and include specific statements by the donor, the attorney, a medical practitioner and a legal practitioner, and must confirm the donor's capacity and understanding of the implications of creating the enduring power of attorney.

Notice of the creation of the EPA must be given to various individuals specified in the legislation[16] as soon as is practicable thereafter, and in the case of EPAs under the 2015 Act an application to register the EPA must be made to the DSS within prescribed time limits.

6.1 A decision-making assistance agreement must:

- be in writing;
- include details of the decisions that the decision-making assistant will include;
- include a statement by the supported person that he or she understands the agreement;
- be signed by the supported person and the decision-making assistant; and
- have confirmation from the decision-making assistant that he or she understands and will carry out the required duties.

6.2 A co-decision-making agreement must:

- be in writing;
- be signed by the supported person (or on his or her behalf in certain circumstances);
- be signed by the co-decision-maker;
- be witnessed by two other people; and
- be accompanied by a statement of capacity form.[17]

6.3 A Decision-Making Representative Order:

- is obtained on application to the Circuit Court;
- will require medical evidence as to the capacity of the supported person; and
- will require evidence as to the circumstances giving rise to the necessity for a decision-making representative.

7. Is there a registration process for powers of representation?

EPAs made prior to 26 April 2023 must be registered with the Office of Wards of Court by application to the Registrar, Wards of Court, on loss of capacity of the donor.

EPAs made on or after 26 April 2023, Decision-Making Representative Orders and co-decision-making agreements must be registered with the DSS.

A decision-making assistance agreement does not require registration with the DSS but the DSS should be informed and furnished with a copy of the agreement.

8. How can a power of representation be revoked or terminated (ie, in the event of marriage, divorce or death)?

Powers of representation cease to have effect on the death of the donor or the relevant or supported person. Under the 1996 Act an EPA made prior to 26 April 2023, once registered, cannot be revoked except by order of the court.[18] An EPA made under the 2015 Act may be revoked on application to the DSS prior to its activation and coming into effect on the loss of the donor's capacity.

9. Is the process of making and/or registering a power of representation supervised by a court or government body?

EPAs made prior to 26 April 2023 must be registered with the Office of Wards of Court by application to the Registrar, Wards of Court. EPAs made on or after 26 April 2023, Decision-Making Representative Orders and Co-Decision-Making Agreements must be registered with the DSS.

10. Is there a governmental or administrative body with oversight of the validity of a power of representation and supervision of its use?

The DSS has a complaints department where complaints about the management of enduring powers of attorney can be brought. To that extent, the oversight of EPAs, whether created under the 2015 Act or the 1996 Act, falls under the remit of the DSS.

The High Court, however, ultimately remains the venue for any litigation around enduring powers of attorney registered under the 1996 Act.

The director of the DSS has authority to supervise, in accordance with the provisions of the 2015 Act, compliance by decision-making assistants, co-decision-makers, decision-making representatives and attorneys in the performance of their functions under the 2015 Act.[19]

In this context the director of the DSS may appoint and direct a special visitor[20] or general visitor[21] to examine and take copies of any health, personal welfare or financial records held in relation to a relevant person by any person, body or organisation, and to interview a relevant person and their decision supporter.

11. What role do the courts in your jurisdiction have in relation to powers of representation?
For EPAs made under the 1996 Act the High Court, in addition to its inherent jurisdiction, has jurisdiction to deal with issues arising as to the validity of the instrument creating the EPA on the application for its registration to the Registrar, Wards of Court and the High Court remains the venue for any litigation around enduring powers of attorney registered under the 1996 Act.

Under the 2015 Act the Circuit Court is given jurisdiction to appoint a decision-making representative and to review, vary or revoke a Decision-Making Representative Order.

If, during an investigation, instigated by a complaint, it appears the supported person or his or her property is at immediate risk of harm from his or her decision-making assistant, co-decision-maker, decision-making representative, or attorney, the DSS has powers to apply to the court for a temporary prohibition order, pending the outcome of the investigation.

12. Are foreign powers of representation legally recognised in your jurisdiction? If so, what is the applicable legal framework?
Foreign powers of representation are not legally recognised in this jurisdiction. An application can be made to the High Court seeking recognition and registration of a foreign power of representation under Irish law. To succeed, the foreign power of representation will need to comply with requirements for powers of representation as they apply under Irish law.

13. Has your jurisdiction ratified The Hague Convention on the International Protection of Adults 2000? If not, are there any plans to do so in the near future?
Ireland has ratified the international agreement on the protection of adults, known as The Hague Convention on the International Protection of Adults 2000. It was first signed by Ireland on 18 September 2008, and the instrument of ratification was deposited on 31 May 2024. The convention will enter into force in the state from 1 September 2024.

14. Is there any publicly available guidance on the law and procedure concerning powers of representation in your jurisdiction?
The DSS[22] and the Wards of Court Office[23] are useful sources of reference.

Notes

1 See Powers of Attorney Act 1996 (Commencement Order) 1996 (SI 195/1996).
2 See Part III of the 1996 Act.
3 To be found in Part XI of the Conveyancing Act 1881 and Sections 8 and 9 of the Conveyancing Act 1882.
4 See Part II of the 1996 Act.
5 Note that all sections of the Assisted Decision-Making (Capacity) Act 2015 have been commenced and given effect.
6 Assisted Decision-Making (Capacity) Act 2015 (Commencement) Order 2023 (SI 192/2023).
7 See www.irishstatutebook.ie/eli/2015/act/64/section/58/enacted/en/html#part7.
8 The DSS will oversee all decision-making arrangements under the 2015 Act. See https://decisionsupportservice.ie.
9 The person who creates the enduring power of attorney.
10 See www.courts.ie/office-wards-court.
11 The person appointed by the donor to look after his or her financial and/or personal affairs, in the event that the donor no longer has the mental capacity to do so.
12 See HC99 Practice Direction of the High Court Enduring Powers of Attorney – Medical Reports (23 October 2020), www.courts.ie/content/enduring-powers-attorney-medical-reports.
13 Assisted Decision-Making (Capacity) Act 2015, Section 3.
14 For information on Advance Healthcare Directives which are not included, see Section 84 of the Assisted Decision-Making (Capacity) Act 2015.
15 Section 2(1) of the Assisted Decision-Making (Capacity) Act 2015 defines a relevant person as "(a) a person whose capacity is in question or may shortly be in question in respect of one or more than one matter, (b) a person who lacks capacity in respect of one or more than one matter, or (c) a person who falls within paragraphs (a) and (b) at the same time but in respect of different matters."
16 Whether made under the 1996 or the 2015 Acts.
17 The supported person must consult with his or her doctor or another healthcare professional to have an assessment of capacity. If the doctor or healthcare professional deems the person able to make the co-decision-making agreement and to have the capacity to make the decisions included in the proposed agreement, with the support of a co-decision-maker, the doctor will complete the statement of capacity form.
18 Powers of Attorney Act 1996, Section 12(3). On application, on notice to the attorney, made by or on behalf of the donor, the court shall confirm the revocation of the power if satisfied that the donor has done whatever is necessary in law to effect an express revocation of the power and was mentally capable of revoking a power of attorney at the time of the purported revocation.
19 Assisted Decision-Making (Capacity) Act 2015, Section 95(1)(e).
20 For special visitor, see *ibid*, Section 99(2).
21 For general visitor, see *ibid*, Section 99(3).
22 See Decision Support Service, www.decisionsupportservice.ie.
23 See Courts Service, "General Information on Enduring Powers of Attorney", www.courts.ie/general-information-enduring-powers-attorney.

Italy

Martina Moscardi
Caldara & Associati

The Italian Constitution embodies the principles of protecting people with particular regard to those who are vulnerable.[1] Given these assumptions, the Italian jurisdiction also recognises the same principles as pillars of the European legal framework and as part of the wider international law.[2]

According to these basic elements, and for readers' ease of use, we have divided this chapter into in two parts covering legislation dealing with powers of representation:

- that are provided by a private appointment of an attorney; and
- in which the court has the primary role.

I. RELATIONSHIP BETWEEN TWO PRIVATE PARTIES

1. Does your jurisdiction have legislation providing for powers of representation such as ordinary, continuing, enduring or lasting powers of attorney?

Italian legislation provides extensive rules for ordinary powers of representation. The general rule[3] establishes that it is formed as a contract between two parties (the donor and the attorney) in which the latter is appointed:

- for the general management of a person's patrimonial affair; or
- for a specific deal to be concluded, eg, opening a bank account or the purchase or selling of an estate (duration and object should be clearly defined).

Both cases apply only to property (assets) and the contract is effective as long as the donor has full capacity.

2. When do powers of representation come into effect and what are the formalities of establishing a power of representation?

The private appointment of an attorney should be formed in writing. Certain types of deeds – according to Italian law – need to be in the written form (duly signed before the notary) otherwise they are invalid and in certain cases considered non-existent. Therefore, the power of attorney (POA) must be in written form and duly signed by both parties.

The POA must be signed before a public notary who is entitled to certify the signature of the donor. The effects of the power of representation come into effect when the document has been certified by the notary.

The notary will assess the capacity of the donor in order to appoint the attorney and to sign the POA. During this assessment process the notary also verifies the rights of the donor to delegate or not.

3. Is there a registration process for powers of representation?

Public registration is not required. Whenever the attorney is asked to act on behalf of the donor, then he or she shall confirm the power by showing the notary deed.

4. Can a power of representation be revoked or terminated (ie, in the event of marriage, divorce or death)?

A private appointment can be either revoked or terminated in the following situations, provided by law:[4]

- upon termination of the contract (in the case of a general POA);
- when the specific action has been duly performed (in the case of a special POA);
- if revocable and the donor revokes it;
- where the attorney dismisses the power; or
- in the event of death or loss of capacity of the donor or attorney.[5]

5. Does your jurisdiction have a legal test for determining mental capacity?

It is of primary importance to know if the donor is mentally capable and to ensure this capacity remains during the entire duration of the appointment. The notary may wish to refer to qualified medical professionals (eg, a gerontologist) to assess the capacity of the donor before the appointment.

II. POA AND THE ROLE OF THE COURTS

As soon as the donor loses his or her mental capacity, as assessed by qualified medical professionals, any provision regarding the management of assets and the welfare and care is then referred to the court.[6] According to the personal circumstances, and the social and family environment, the court can issue different measures.

1. What role do the courts in your jurisdiction have in relation to powers of representation?[7]

In cases where a total lack of capacity is involved the court can appoint an attorney to act on behalf of the incapacitated person.[8]

This is similar to a lasting power of attorney (LPA) and a guardianship in which someone is given the right – and the duty – to make decisions about financial and legal affairs, or to decide about health and welfare care. The main powers and duties rely on the general needs and protection of the person. The attorney is accountable to the incapacitated person and generally to the court in case of abuse, neglect or fraud. A family member or a professional can be appointed, depending on the nature of activities to be carried out.

In the case of diminished capacity, even severe, the court can issue a restrictive provision which appoints a guardian/manager to act, temporarily or permanently, on behalf of and for the benefit of the incapacitated person[9] in relation to assets and for general care. The appointed guardian shall also support the incapacitated person to carry on some minor or particular activities which he or she is still able to perform. Further:

- the court can choose to nominate family members or certified professionals; or
- the choice may have been made in advance by the incapacitated person by way of a notarised deed duly certified. In this case, the incapacitated person can also leave instructions in relation to future business affairs and wealth or care decisions. The guardian is also accountable to the court.

In both cases the appointed representative can be revoked and substituted if he or she is no longer suitable for the role. The LPA ends with the death of the incapacitated person. The attorney or the guardian cannot be a beneficiary of the will of the incapacitated person unless there is a family relationship between them.

2. What are the formalities of establishing this kind of power of representation?

According to the provisions, the court establishes the list of rights and activities to be undertaken. In the event that further needs arise, the appointed representative can apply to the court for authorisation. The court oversees the report on an annual basis or whenever is appropriate.

3. Is there a registration process for powers of representation?

LPAs are mentioned in the Court Register and supervised periodically.

4. Are there any other protective measures available?

Trusts are often used in Italy to protect the assets of incapacitated persons (adults and minors) and to provide more flexible powers to the trustee and protector. Trusts are recognised as a suitable legal tool in cases where family assets need to be managed and transferred within family if a member is incapacitated.[10]

5. Are foreign powers of representation legally recognised in your jurisdiction? If so, what is the applicable legal framework?

Italian private international law[11] provides a set of rules according to different situations, such as:

- when a POA has not been established but there is an urgent need to protect the local assets of a foreign person or to protect, in Italy, the foreign owner;[12]
- when a foreign court (Court of Protection or Family Court) issued an LPA and it needs to be effective in Italy (eg, assets located in Italy, succession process in which Italian law applies);[13] and
- when a private person formed an LPA or enduring power of attorney (EPA) and the attorney needs to have it recognised in Italy.[14]

In the first case, the Italian court can directly intervene to protect and give directions for the best interests of the person and the assets; in the second one, the attorney can apply to the court which is entitled to check that the person's rights have been protected in a fair process and then it recognises the POA; in the last case, there are strict rules about formality and certification of the signatures. That means that an LPA or EPA can be so construed into Italian jurisdiction by the 'mutual recognition' principle.[15]

6. Has your jurisdiction ratified The Hague Convention on the International Protection of Adults 2000? If not, are there any plans for your jurisdiction to do so in the near future?

Unfortunately, not yet. But ratification is ongoing and there is a draft bill (DDL 789/2023)[16] to be discussed by Parliament.

There is also a proposal for a Regulation of the European Parliament and of the Council "on jurisdiction, applicable law, recognition and enforcement of measures and cooperation in matters relating to the protection of adults"[17] in which the basic principles of the convention are to be embodied and harmonised among the member states.

7. Is there any publicly available guidance on the law and procedure concerning powers of representation in your jurisdiction?

Besides the Civil Code rules and the related relevant case law, to be carefully handled by professionals, special guides can be found at www.notariato.it and www.giustizia.it.

Notes

1 OJ No 289 (27 December 1947), Articles 2, 3 and 32.
2 For example, OJ No 61 (14 March 2009); Law No 18 (3 March 2009), Articles 1 and 2, ratifying the UN Convention on the Rights of Persons with Disabilities (New York, 13 December 2006).
3 Article 1387 of the Civil Code.
4 Article 1722 of the Civil Code.
5 Article 1723 of the Civil Code for the exemption rule regarding the *ultra vires* powers of the attorney.
6 *Tribunale civile sezione Volontaria Giurisdizione*, "Inherent Jurisdiction of the Court for the protection of persons".
7 Cass civ, Sez I, Ordinanza No 32219 (21 November 2023).
8 Articles 414 and 415 of the Civil Code.
9 Article 1 L No 6 (9 January 2004), "Amministrazione di sostegno": "This law aims to protect, with the least possible limitation of the capacity to act, persons deprived in whole or in part of autonomy in the performance of the functions of daily living, by means of temporary or permanent support interventions".
10 Law No 112 (22 June 2016), in OJ No 146 (24 June 2016), Article 1, "scope".
11 Law No 218 (31 May 1995), in OJ No 128 (3 June 1995).
12 *Ibid*, Articles 9 and 44.
13 *Ibid*, Articles 65, 66 and 67.
14 *Ibid*, Article 68.
15 *Ibid*, Article 60, "reciprocal principle" and "mutual recognition" of a foreign POA.
16 See www.governo.it/it/provvedimento/provvedimento-a35032425o5233/22748, XIX LEGISLATURA – DISEGNI DI LEGGE E RELAZIONI – DOCUMENTI, Senato della Repubblica No 789.
17 European Commission (31 May 2023), COM (2023) 280 final: Explanatory Memorandum, p2: "While the rules in the Convention are aimed at a global application by countries with different legal systems in general and on the protection of adults in particular, the Regulation would be able to establish more streamlined rules and closer cooperation based on the principle of mutual trust among Member States and drawing on the experience of harmonising other areas of cross-border civil justice in the EU. It follows that the proposed Regulation would apply among Member States, while the HCCH 2000 Protection of Adults Convention would be applicable in relation to non-EU countries that are Contracting Parties to the Convention". At https://op.europa.eu/it/publication-detail/-/publication.

Jersey

Stephen Alexander
Joel Evans
Mourant

1. Does your jurisdiction have legislation providing for powers of representation such as ordinary, continuing, enduring or lasting powers of attorney?

The two main statutes dealing with the provision of powers of attorney in Jersey are the Powers of Attorney (Jersey) Law 1995 (the POA Law) and the Capacity and Self-Determination (Jersey) Law 2016 (the Capacity Law). The POA Law provides the statutory framework for general powers of attorney (GPA) and the Capacity Law provides the statutory framework for lasting powers of attorney (LPA).

In Jersey, GPAs are often used to grant a donee the power to assist the donor with everyday matters such as paying a bill or assisting with the completion of income tax assessments. An LPA differs from a GPA in that it can survive the incapacity of the donor, whereas a GPA cannot. In addition, GPAs cannot be granted in respect of a donor's health/welfare whereas an LPA can. In short, under Jersey law, LPAs have a much wider scope than GPAs.

2. When do powers of representation come into effect?

Article 2(2) of the POA Law details that a GPA takes effect upon it being "duly executed", unless the power of attorney states otherwise. Article 2(3) of the POA Law provides that a GPA is duly executed if it is "signed by the donor, or acknowledged by the donor to have been signed by the donor in the presence of one witness who is not a party to the power of attorney".

Article 2(4) of the POA Law details that a power of attorney may be executed without any further attestation by a "body corporate in the manner permitted by its articles of association" and a "limited liability company in the manner permitted by its LLC agreement as defined in Article 1(1) of the Limited Liability (Jersey) Law 2018".

Article 3 of the POA Law introduces the concept of "registrable powers of attorney" for a power of attorney which is defined under Article 3(a) as a power of attorney that is "intended to be used to effect a transaction which is required to be registered" or "required to be registered by any enactment other than a provision of this law". An application to register a registrable power of attorney needs to be made to the Royal Court.

Article 13(1)(a) of the Capacity Law details that an LPA is not validly created unless "the instrument purporting to create it complies with the requirements of this Part, and with the requirements as to execution in, and prescribed under, Part 1 of the Schedule" and "it is registered by the Judicial Greffe in accordance with the requirements as to registration in Part 2 of the Schedule". An LPA will therefore come into effect once it has been validly created and registered with the Judicial Greffe.

3. Does your jurisdiction have a legal test for determining mental capacity?

Articles 4 and 5 of the Capacity Law provide the statutory basis for assessing mental capacity under Jersey law.

Article 4(1) of the Capacity Law provides that a person lacks capacity if "(a) the person is unable to make his or her own decision in relation to the matter" because "(b) he or she suffers from an impairment or a disturbance in the functioning of his or her mind or brain".

Article 5(1) of the Capacity Law states that for the purposes of Article 4(1), a person is unable to make his or her own decision if he or she cannot "understand information relevant to that decision, retain the information for a period, however short, which is sufficient to make the decision; use or weigh the information in making the decision; or communicate the decision (whether by speech, sign language, or any other means)".

The test for mental capacity under Jersey law is therefore formed of three parts comprising Articles 4(1)(a), (b) and 5(1)(a) of the Capacity Law.

4. Can the powers of representation deal with property and finances and/or health and welfare?

A GPA will allow a donee to do, on the donor's behalf, anything he or she can lawfully do by an attorney, save for those functions for which the donor has a trustee or personal representative. This includes matters relating to an individual's finances but excludes those relating to health and welfare. A registrable power of attorney is required for matters relating to property transactions.

Article 11(2)(a) and (b) of the Capacity Law provides the means for two types of LPA in Jersey. The first concerns health and welfare and the second concerns property and affairs. Under a Health and Welfare LPA, the donor is able to appoint an attorney to make decisions in relation to his or her medical health which permits the attorney to deal with a variety of issues such as managing the donor's daily health routine and making decisions in relation to the refusal or continuation of life-sustaining treatment. A Health and Welfare LPA will only be operational in circumstances where the donor is no longer able to make decisions regarding such issues for his or herself.

A Property and Affairs LPA permits the attorney to undertake any action that a donor could lawfully do for his or herself in relation to his or her property and affairs. Article 15(2) of the Capacity Law does, however, put some restrictions on an attorney making gifts and provides that "Subject to any conditions or restrictions in the instrument", an attorney "may make gifts of P's property – (a) on customary occasions to persons (including A) who are related to or connected with P; and (b) to any charity to which P made gifts or might have been expected to make gifts, if the value of each such gift is not unreasonable having regard to all the circumstances and in particular to the size of P's estate". It is also important to note that, unlike a Health and Welfare LPA, under a Property and Affairs LPA, the attorney may also act while the donor still possesses mental capacity.

5. Are there any other protective measures available?

In circumstances where an individual loses mental capacity and does not have an LPA, an application can be made to the Royal Court under Article 24(2)(a) of the Capacity Law to either "make a decision on P's behalf as to the matter" or Article 24(2)(b) to "appoint a delegate to make a decision on P's behalf as to such matters".

If a delegate is appointed on behalf of an individual, the delegate will be able to make a variety of decisions in relation to that individual's affairs.

Article 35(1) confers a wide range of powers onto a delegate who (subject to any restriction or condition imposed by the court) may "do, or secure the doing of, anything which appears to the delegate to be necessary or expedient to be done in P's best interests".

In cases where a delegate is appointed to deal with an individual's property or affairs, the power conferred on a delegate under Article 35 of the Capacity Law includes the "power to do or secure the doing of anything necessary or expedient – (a) for the maintenance or other benefit of P, P's family or dependents [*sic*]; and (b) for the payment of P's debts, whether legally enforceable or not".

Article 35(4) of the Capacity Law makes it clear that a delegate must act in the best interests of the individual and the delegate's actions are supervised by the Royal Court.

6. What are the formalities of establishing a power of representation?

A GPA will take effect upon it being duly executed (signed by the donor in the presence of one witness who is not a party to the power of attorney). A registrable power of attorney requires the presence of a specific class of witness described in Article 3(2)(a) and (b) of the POA Law alongside an application to the Royal Court.

Notwithstanding the above, it is possible for a GPA and registrable power of attorney to be valid, even in circumstances where it has not been signed by the donor. This is possible if the requirements listed in Article 3A of the POA Law are met. These requirements are: 3A(a) "the donor declared in the presence of a qualified witness that, being physically incapacitated to sign the power of attorney himself or herself, the donor wished the power of attorney to be signed by another person on the donor's behalf"; 3A(b) "the declaration by the donor and the date it was made are recorded on the face of the power of attorney"; 3A(c) "the power of attorney was read aloud to the donor (or, in the case of a deaf donor, the whole contents of the power of attorney were made known to the donor by some other means) in the presence of the person signing the power of attorney on behalf of the donor and the qualified witness"; and 3A(d) "after the power of attorney was read to the donor (or, in the case of a deaf donor, after the whole contents of the power of attorney were made known to him or her by some other means), it was signed by some other person on the donor's behalf in the presence of a qualified witness and that witness put his or her signature to the power of attorney in the presence of the donor and that other person".

The process for registering an LPA is detailed in Part 1 of Schedule 1 of the Capacity Law. The donor (or his or her lawyer or agent) must complete the requisite online form in preparation of the relevant signatures.

The donor must be accompanied by a professional witness (such as a lawyer or a doctor) who is required to witness the donor's signature and certify that the donor has the mental capacity to make the LPA and that they are not acting under undue influence. The attorneys must also sign the LPA which confirms their acceptance of their duties under it.

A corporate entity or a professional person may be an attorney and an attorney must be over the age of 18 and (in relation to a Property and Affairs LPA) must not be bankrupt. The attorney must have regard to the Code of Practice issued pursuant to the Capacity Law.

Article 12(2) of the Capacity Law permits the appointment of more than one attorney to act alongside one another. The donor must decide whether the attorneys are to be appointed to act jointly in all decisions (requiring them to agree and sign all the relevant documents in order to validate a decision) or whether the attorneys may act severally (so that one may act alone). Under Jersey law, the attorneys can act jointly in relation to some decisions and alone in relation to others. In addition, Article 12(5)(b) of the Capacity Law permits a donor to appoint substitute attorneys in the LPA who can take over from first choice attorneys in circumstances where they are unable to act (because of illness, death or absence).

7. Is there a registration process for powers of representation?

A GPA will take effect upon it being duly executed, however, a registrable power of attorney is not exercisable until it has been duly executed and registered in the Public Registry.

Part 2 of Schedule 1 of the Capacity Law details that an LPA must be registered in the prescribed form available online from the Judicial Greffe. Once all the relevant signatures and certifications have been completed, the signed form must be registered with the Probate and Protection Department of the Judicial Greffe together with a payment of £25 in order to make the LPA legally binding.

8. How can a power of representation be revoked or terminated (ie, in the event of marriage, divorce or death)?

Article 9(1) of the POA Law details that a GPA "may be revoked or abandoned by a document conforming generally to whichever of the forms in Schedule 3 is applicable and executed in the same manner as is required for the creation of a power of attorney under this Law". Article 9(5) of the POA Law details that a GPA is also revoked by the "death, incapacity or bankruptcy of the donor or, if the donor is a body corporate or limited liability company, by its bankruptcy or dissolution".

Article 17 of the Capacity Law details the means by which an LPA can be revoked. In Jersey, an LPA will be terminated upon the death or revocation by the donor. An LPA may also terminate in circumstances where the attorney becomes bankrupt (in relation to a Property and Affairs LPA only), mentally incapacitated, deceased or divorces or annuls a civil partnership with the donor. The Royal Court may also terminate an LPA if it finds that the attorney has acted inappropriately, and it is in the best interests of the donor to revoke the LPA.

9. Is the process of making and/or registering a power of representation supervised by a court or government body?

The Probate and Protection Department of the Judicial Greffe is the body responsible for administering the registration of powers of attorney in Jersey. The Judicial Greffe is a court department which provides judicial, secretarial, administrative and interlocutory support for the courts and tribunals of Jersey.

10. Is there a governmental or administrative body with oversight of the validity of a power of representation and supervision of its use?

The Probate and Protection Department of the Judicial Greffe is the body responsible for administering the registration of powers of attorney in Jersey.

The Royal Court has various powers in relation to the validity and operation of an LPA which will be discussed in further detail in the following question.

11. What role do the courts in your jurisdiction have in relation to powers of representation?

The Royal Court has various powers in relation to the validity and operation of an LPA which are detailed in Articles 19 and 20 of the Capacity Law.

Article 19(1) of the Capacity Law deals with the powers of the court in relation to the validity of an LPA and it states that the court may determine any question as to whether "(a) one or more of the requirements for the creation of a lasting power of attorney have been met; or (b) a lasting power of attorney has been revoked or otherwise come to an end".

Article 20(1) of the Capacity Law deals with the operation of an LPA and details that "The Court may determine any question as to the meaning or effect of a lasting power of attorney or of any instrument purporting to confer authority by a lasting power of attorney".

Article 20(2) provides that the court may give directions with "(a) respect to a decision which is within the authority conferred on A by a lasting power of attorney, if P lacks capacity to make the decision; and (b) as to – (i) the rendering of reports or accounts by A and the production of records kept by A for the purpose of such reports or accounts, (ii) A's renumeration or expenses".

Article 20(3) of the Capacity Law enables the court to authorise the making of certain gifts by an attorney who otherwise would have had to obtain permission from the donor to give such a gift (if the donor had capacity).

Article 20(4) of the Capacity Law enables the court to require the attorney to "produce documents or any other things, which are within A's possession as a result of the authority conferred on A by a lasting power of attorney" and Article 20(5) permits the court to relieve an attorney "wholly or partly from any liability which A has or may have incurred as a result of breach of duties imposed on A by a lasting power of attorney".

12. Are foreign powers of representation legally recognised in your jurisdiction? If so, what is the applicable legal framework?
Royal Court Practice Direction RC22/03 provides that "applications for the registration of LPAs (*or the equivalent thereof*) originally registered outside of the British Islands must be commenced by a Representation". The Jersey court will therefore recognise a foreign power of attorney (or equivalent) provided that it is registered with the Royal Court. Once registered and confirmed by a formal Act of Court, the attorney appointed under the foreign document will then have the legal authority to deal with the donor's affairs in Jersey.

The application to register a foreign power of attorney is made by a representation which is an application made by a Jersey qualified lawyer who must provide:

- the original (registered) LPA (or equivalent document) or a copy of that document that has been officially sealed and certified by the court in the foreign jurisdiction that registered the original;
- confirmation of the current value of the asset or assets in Jersey (eg, a bank statement or share valuation or similar);
- identification documents from both the donor and the attorney; and
- a £330 registration fee.

In addition, if a foreign power of attorney (or equivalent) is not required to be formally registered in the country of origin in order for it to be officially valid and utilised (and therefore the requirement listed in the first bullet point above cannot be met), then it will also require an affidavit from a lawyer in that jurisdiction which confirms this.

13. Has your jurisdiction ratified The Hague Convention on the International Protection of Adults 2000? If not, are there any plans for your jurisdiction to do so in the near future?

Jersey has not ratified The Hague Convention on the International Protection of Adults 2000 and the authors are not aware of any immediate plans which suggest that this is likely to change.

14. Is there any publicly available guidance on the law and procedure concerning powers of representation in your jurisdiction?

The Government of Jersey website (www.gov.je/pages/default.aspx) contains useful information which details the process of making and registering an LPA. The website provides an overview of the Capacity Law and explains what an LPA is, alongside how one can be made. Similarly, Citizens Advice Jersey (a charitable organisation which offers impartial advice to members of the public) has produced a useful free guide in relation to the setting up of an LPA.

Malaysia

Farah Deba Mohamed Sofian
Wong Lu Peen & Tunku Alina

1. Does your jurisdiction have legislation providing for powers of representation such as ordinary, continuing, enduring or lasting powers of attorney?

Malaysia does not have laws which recognise the concept of continuing, enduring or lasting powers of attorney as practised by countries like the United Kingdom and Singapore. Malaysian laws on powers of attorney (POA) are contained exclusively in the Powers of Attorney Act 1949 (POA 1949) which applies only to the states of West Malaysia.

The powers granted by a donor generally are not perpetual in nature. In Malaysia, powers granted to an attorney continue to be in force only until the donor or donee has been adjudged to be of unsound mind. This means the power so granted ends on his or her unsoundness of mind.

There are exceptions. The circumstances upon which POAs continue to be in force and irrevocable despite unsoundness of mind of the donor is limited to the following:

- if the POA is expressly stated as given for valuable consideration; or
- if the POA expressly specifies a fixed time (whether given for valuable consideration or not);

then the power shall not be revoked in favour of a purchaser. This suggests that only in the case of a sale transaction can a POA be irrevocable and surpass the donor's mental capacity. This also means that in any other case the same POA ceases to have any effect and cannot be used by the appointed attorney.

2. When do powers of representation come into effect?

An instrument creating a POA will only come into effect once it has been deposited at the Power of Attorney Registration Office at any High Court of Malaya.

3. Does your jurisdiction have a legal test for determining mental capacity?

Current laws to determine mental capacity can be found in the Mental Health Act 2001. It stipulates that only the court has the power to determine whether a person is mentally disordered or not. An individual can petition the court for an inquiry to ascertain whether a person is unable to manage his or her affairs due to a mental disorder. The court will then assess the evidence presented to determine the person's capacity to manage his or her own personal and legal affairs. Unless otherwise dispensed with, the court will generally only recognise the medical report of a psychiatrist from the Malaysian government hospital to determine the state of mental health of a person alleged to be mentally incapacitated.

In the case of *Lim Siew Kim v Kien Huat Realty Sdn Bhd & Anor*,[1] the court is not persuaded by the plaintiff's claim of mental incapacity because there is no medical evidence being submitted before the court to support the claim. The court is of the view that it falls within the purview of a medical expert to determine whether a person is mentally incapacitated.

4. Can the powers of representation deal with property and finances and/or health and welfare?

There are no specific provisions in the POA 1949 prohibiting or detailing out the scope and power to be granted to an attorney. It can therefore be said that the powers to be granted to an attorney can include the power to deal with a donor's property, financial and legal matters, and his or her personal affairs and health.

It is to be noted, however, that where health is concerned, but related to medical decision making, due to the limitation in the laws of POA, the advanced medical directive (AMD) is the alternative practice. It is made when a person is competent "regarding his future medical treatment in the event that he becomes incapable of decision making when the need arises. It consists of anticipatory instructions and decisions as to the extent of treatment that a person agrees or refuses to receive and may also include the appointment of a proxy who is authorised to make healthcare decisions on the person's behalf".[2] An AMD is understood by some to function similarly to a lasting power of attorney, though its purview is strictly limited to medical decisions only.

Clause 5 of Section II of the Code of Medical Ethics of the Malaysian Medical Association (CME) states that in the case of a dying patient, "one should always take into consideration any advance directives and the wishes of the family in this regard".[3] While the code of ethics appears to be persuasive in nature, it is not binding. Since there are no established laws protecting medical practitioners from AMD implementation, it is known that medical practitioners will still consult and obtain the agreement of the next of kin.

5. Are there any other protective measures available?

There are none available.

6. What are the formalities of establishing a power of representation?

It is imperative that powers of attorney to be deemed validly executed and attested must conform to the form and substance as provided for in the POA 1949. All instruments creating powers of attorney must contain the authentication clause as follows:

- in the case of a power of attorney executed by an individual:
  I .... (Magistrate, Justice of the Peace, Land Administrator, Notary Public, Commissioner for Oaths, Bank Official or Advocate and Solicitor of the High Court in Malaya) officiating [or practising] at ...., hereby certify that the donor above named was in my presence on this .... day of .... 20 ...., and is, to my own personal knowledge, [or according to information given to me by trustworthy and respectable persons, namely .... of .... and .... of ...., which information I verily believe,] the truth of .... who has acknowledged to me that he is of full age and that he has voluntarily executed this instrument.

  Witness my hand ....

- in the case of a power of attorney executed by a company or corporation:
  I .... (Magistrate, Justice of the Peace, Land Administrator, Notary Public, Commissioner for Oaths, Bank Official or Advocate and Solicitor of the High Court in Malaya) officiating [or practising] at ...., hereby certify that on this .... day of .... 20 ...., the common seal of (state name of company or corporation) was duly affixed to the above written instrument

in my presence in accordance with the regulations of the said company/corporation.

Witness my hand ....

Only the persons specified under the POA 1949 are empowered to attest powers of attorney. If executed within West Malaysia, by any one of the following:

- a magistrate;
- a justice of the peace;
- a land administrator;
- a notary public;
- a commissioner for oaths;
- an advocate and solicitor; or
- an officer, acting in the course of his or her employment, of a company carrying on the business of banking in West Malaysia and incorporated by or under any written law in force in West Malaysia.

If executed outside West Malaysia, by any one of the following:

- a notary public;
- a commissioner for oaths;
- a judge;
- a magistrate;
- a British consul or vice-consul;
- a representative of His British Majesty;
- on and after Merdeka Day, any consular officer of Malaysia;
- in the case of an instrument executed in the Kingdom of Saudi Arabia, the Malaysian Pilgrimage Commissioner; or
- in the case of an instrument executed in the Republic of Singapore, an advocate and solicitor of the Supreme Court of the Republic; or an officer, acting in the course of his or her employment, of a company carrying on the business of banking in the Republic and incorporated by or under any written law of the Republic.

7. Is there a registration process for powers of representation?
A POA must be stamped, the original and duplicate copies of which must be deposited in court for registration.

In the case of *Adam Karpen & Anor v Kumari Geethavani Perumal*,[4] it was held that the instrument was invalid and unenforceable because the POA should have been deposited and registered at the High Court of Malaya during the lifetime of the donor. Failing to do so will render the POA invalid and unenforceable.

Where the power granted is in relation to land, it must be registered with the relevant land registry.

8. How can a power of representation be revoked or terminated (ie, in the event of marriage, divorce or death)?

A POA may be revoked unilaterally by revocation by the donor or renunciation by the donee and must be deposited in every office where a copy of the POA has been deposited.

Notwithstanding the above, a POA is also revoked upon:

- the death of the donor or donee;
- the unsoundness of mind of the donor or donee; or
- the bankruptcy of a donor.

9. Is the process of making and/or registering a power of representation supervised by a court or government body?

There is no legal framework in Malaysia for the court or any other governmental body to supervise the process of making or registering a POA. The court serves only as a depository and registry function.

10. Is there a governmental or administrative body with oversight of the validity of a power of representation and supervision of its use?

There is no governmental or administrative body to oversee the validity of a POA in Malaysia.

In practice, financial institutions or land authorities may, however, require a statutory declaration to be furnished by the donor that the power of attorney so granted has not been revoked and remains to be valid.

11. What role do the courts in your jurisdiction have in relation to powers of representation?

The court serves only as a registry body for the registration of a POA that has been deposited in court.

12. Are foreign powers of representation legally recognised in your jurisdiction? If so, what is the applicable legal framework?

There is no legal framework in Malaysia to recognise foreign powers of representation. All POAs must be executed and deposited in accordance with the POA 1949.

13. Has your jurisdiction ratified The Hague Convention on the International Protection of Adults 2000? If not, are there any plans for your jurisdiction to do so in the near future?

Malaysia is not a party to The Hague Convention on International

Protection of Adults 2000. However, medical and legal practitioners in Malaysia have been active in calling for a change in the laws on POA and the introduction of mental capacity laws.

14. Is there any publicly available guidance on the law and procedure concerning powers of representation in your jurisdiction?

There is privately issued literature but there is no publicly available guidance issued at the governmental level.

Notes

1 [2023] 3 MLRH 646.
2 Alexander Morgan Capron, "Advance Directives", in *A Companion to Bioethics*, ed. Helga Kuhse and Peter Singer, 2nd edition (West Sussex: John Wiley & Sons, 2009), pp299–311 at p299, quoted in Puteri Nemie Jahn Kassim and Fadhlina Alias, "Advance Directives for Medical Treatment: The Current Legal Status", *The Malayan Law Journal* [2015] 3 MLJ, ii–iii.
3 Code of Medical Ethics of the Malaysian Medical Association (CME).
4 [2021] MLRHU 2144.

New Zealand

Martin Haanen
Castle Trustees Ltd

1. Does your jurisdiction have legislation providing for powers of representation such as ordinary, continuing, enduring or lasting powers of attorney?
Yes, New Zealand has the following powers of representation:

- the power of attorney (POA) under common law, a simple contract which is only effective when the donor has mental capacity. In the event of mental incapacity, it is not continuing, enduring or durable and is not effective;
- an enduring power of attorney (EPA) for property (assets); and
- an enduring power of attorney (EPA) for personal care and welfare.

Both types of EPA for property and personal care and welfare are governed in New Zealand by the Protection of Personal and Property Rights Act 1988 (PPPR Act).

2. When do powers of representation come into effect?
An EPA for property (assets) is a private appointment of an attorney by the donor. The attorney can be any adult person. The donor makes a choice when giving this power to the attorney, that the attorney can either act immediately or only in the event of mental incapacity.

'Effective immediately' means that the attorney can act even if the donor has mental capacity. Typically, this is chosen when the donor trusts the attorney and intends that if the donor is debilitated in some way, but still mentally competent, the attorney can act. If the attorney acts, he or she will be asked to provide a self-declared document, called a 'certificate of non-revocation', which confirms that the appointment as attorney is still active. If the donor is still mentally capable and the attorney acts, the attorney is expected to keep the donor informed of what has been done.

'Effective only in the event of mental incapacity' means the EPA lies dormant until the donor is medically assessed as being mentally incapable. Generally, where service providers are dealing with the attorney, they will ask whether the EPA has been 'activated'. The evidence for activation is usually a letter from a medical professional(s) attesting to the mental incapacity of the donor.

An EPA for personal care and welfare is a private appointment of an attorney by a donor who may decide to make the following choice: 'Effective only in the event of mental incapacity'. In this situation:

- the EPA lies dormant until the donor is formally assessed as being mentally incapable;
- the EPA for personal care and welfare assumes the donor, while mentally capable, shall not be overruled by the attorney having given his or her decision, but only in the event of mental incapacity; and
- generally, where service providers are dealing with the attorney they will ask whether the EPA has been 'activated'. The evidence for activation is usually a letter from a medical professional(s) attesting to the mental incapacity of the donor.

A court appointment of a property manager over a subject person (person subject to a property order prescribed in the interpretation section of the PPPR Act), whether voluntary or imposed, is effective on the terms the court sets out. An independent lawyer is appointed to act for the subject person and shall usually recommend to the court appropriate courses of action, for example, pay any creditors, sell a house, make a will etc. The property manager is usually limited to dealing with assets, but in certain circumstances may at a practical level deal with choosing a residential care facility for the donor, even though this technically falls to the attorney with personal care and welfare.

3. Does your jurisdiction have a legal test for determining mental capacity?

No. Tests are carried out by appropriately qualified medical professionals based on the need and scope of the assessment required. They are tailored to the person's needs and are not a tick box or standardised approach, which are used in some jurisdictions.

4. Can the powers of representation deal with property and finances and/or health and welfare?

There are two types of EPA:

- EPA for property (assets) – often the attorney pays bills, deals with investments, selling real estate and residential care costs; and
- EPA for personal care and welfare – often the attorney chooses residential care facilities and/or advises health care workers, usually in long-term care cases, about what the subject person or donor would have liked and disliked medically or health wise, a quasi-patient advocate role.

5. Are there any other protective measures available?

Yes. The attorney can apply to the court for directions. Also, a third party, usually a family member, can apply to the court if required.

The EPA can specify the appointment of a particular person(s) that the attorney must consult with as the donor may decide in relation to, for example:

- accounting, legal and investment advice and bill payments; and
- medical care, residential care and health oversight.

In the event of mental incapacity, the type of medical practitioners who may carry out the assessment could be a GP, neuro-specialist or gerontologist, among others.

6. What are the formalities of establishing a power of representation?

A private EPA requires the donor to seek advice and engage a lawyer, a legal executive (supervised by a lawyer), or a statutory trustee company (approved employee in that company).

The form of the EPA to be used should be used in accordance with the regulations of the PPPR Act, but in some cases law firms have chosen to draft their own form. The form must be prepared and authorised by a lawyer, a legal executive (supervised by a lawyer), or a statutory trustee company (approved employee in that company). There are high levels of advice and liability associated with the preparation and execution of the EPA document. The authoriser will also 'legally' assess the capacity of the donor to sign the EPA, as the legal decision regarding the transfer of decision-making power by an adult to another is treated very seriously.

There is no registration process or register of EPAs in New Zealand. The PPPR Act intended that they are a private arrangement to the parties concerned. However, in the circumstances where a property manager is appointed, and has the same powers as an attorney, they and the subject person are overseen directly by the courts.

The EPA must be explained and executed by the donor in front of the authoriser in a particular and prescribed manner. The donor's attorney must also sign it before a separate witness in a prescribed manner.

7. Is there a registration process for powers of representation?

No. There is no registration process or register of EPAs in New Zealand. The PPPR Act intended that they are a private arrangement to the parties concerned. However, in the circumstances where a property manager is appointed, and has the same powers as an attorney, they and the subject person are overseen directly by the courts. This is a fallback position where the state can get involved if it needs to, but is not a public register.

8. Can a power of representation be revoked or terminated (ie, in the event of marriage, divorce or death)?

A private EPA can be revoked by the donor, while the attorney still has capacity, by making a simple signed and dated declaration revoking the appointment of the attorney and delivering it to the attorney. An EPA ends and has no authority or effect after the death of the donor.

9. Is the process of making and/or registering a power of representation supervised by a court or government body?

The Family Court has oversight of the PPPR Act and disputes may be taken to that court. The PPPR Act provides the format, initiation and execution process to create a legal EPA, as well as the remedies and administration-related provisions.

10. Is there a governmental or administrative body with oversight of the validity of a power of representation and supervision of its use?

Generally, a private EPA is not registered or reported to any official body.

The Family Court has oversight if an EPA is questioned. However, a legal action would have to be initiated against the attorney or on behalf of the donor or subject person if under a property manager. Usually this is where there are concerns of abuse, neglect, fraud or where the attorney is suspected of not acting in the best interests of the donor or subject person.

The state, via the court, can appoint a property manager who is then required to report to the court registrar from the date of appointment:

- within three months, an assessment of the assets of the subject person; and
- within one and two years, an annual report of assets, income and payments.

At three years there is a full review and decision on whether the property manager's appointment should be renewed. Reports are subject to a simple audit by the Public Trust, a statutory trustee.

11. What role do the courts in your jurisdiction have in relation to powers of representation?

The courts can remove and appoint attorneys and property managers. They can also direct the attorney or property manager to:

- make and approve a will for the subject person;
- direct that assets be sold;
- direct that creditors be paid; and
- direct other parties to be involved or removed.

12. Are foreign powers of representation legally recognised in your jurisdiction? If so, what is the applicable legal framework?

Both private and state organisations may choose to recognise a foreign power of representation, based entirely on their own recognisance. If not recognised, the foreign attorney may have to apply to the New Zealand courts and have their power ratified by either the Family Court or the High Court referring to the applicable legislation.

13. Has your jurisdiction ratified The Hague Convention on the International Protection of Adults 2000? If not, are there any plans for your jurisdiction to do so in the near future?

No, and future plans are unknown.

14. Is there any publicly available guidance on the law and procedure concerning powers of representation in your jurisdiction?

The following public guidance is available:

- NZ Govt, PPPR Act Parliament Amendment Bill – foreword: www.parliament.nz/en/pb/hansard-debates/rhr/document/48HansD_20061207_00001158/protection-of-personal-and-property-rights-amendment-bill.
- NZ Govt, PPPR Act: www.legislation.govt.nz/act/public/1988/0004/latest/whole.html.
- *Guidelines for Counsel for subject person appointed under the PPPRA*: www.justice.govt.nz/assets/fc-guidelines-counsel-for-subject-person-pppra.pdf.
- NZ Govt, The court and enduring power of attorney: www.justice.govt.nz/family/powers-to-make-decisions/the-court-and-enduring-power-of-attorney-epa/.

- NZ Govt, The court and enduring power of attorney – forms and explanation: www.justice.govt.nz/assets/epa-in-relation-to-personal-care-and-welfare.docx; www.justice.govt.nz/assets/standard-explanation-epa-personal-care-and-welfare.pdf; www.justice.govt.nz/assets/epa-in-relation-to-property-2021.docx; www.justice.govt.nz/assets/standard-explanation-epa-property.pdf.
- NZ Govt, Enduring Power of Attorney for personal care and welfare: www.govt.nz/browse/family-and-whanau/enduring-power-of-attorney-epa-for-personal-care-and-welfare/.
- NZ Govt, Enduring Power of Attorney for property: www.govt.nz/browse/family-and-whanau/enduring-power-of-attorney-epa-for-property/.
- NZ Govt, Office for Seniors, Creating an enduring power of attorney: https://officeforseniors.govt.nz/our-work/promoting-enduring-power-of-attorney/how-to-create-an-enduring-power-of-attorney/.
- Age Concern, Enduring Power of Attorney: www.ageconcern.org.nz/Public/Public/Info/Money_and_Legal/Enduring_Power_of_Attorney.aspx.
- NZ Law Society, Powers of Attorney: www.lawsociety.org.nz/for-the-public/common-legal-issues/powers-of-attorney/.
- Community Law Centre, Enduring powers of attorney: Planning ahead by choosing someone to make decisions for you: https://communitylaw.org.nz/community-law-manual/chapter-10-decision-making-and-powers-of-attorney/enduring-powers-of-attorney-planning-ahead-by-choosing-someone-to-make-decisions-for-you/how-to-create-an-enduring-power-of-attorney-epa/.

Scotland

Kevin J Winters
Brodies LLP

1. Does your jurisdiction have legislation providing for powers of representation such as ordinary, continuing, enduring or lasting powers of attorney?

In Scotland it is possible to grant two different types of 'power of representation', known as 'power of attorney' (POA):

- POAs granted for a specific act/time period on behalf of the granter, eg, to sign documents on behalf of the granter; and
- POAs to facilitate someone else managing the property and financial affairs and/or personal welfare of the granter.

The latter are governed by and must comply with the Adults with Incapacity (Scotland) Act 2000 (the 2000 Act) and are the subject of further discussion below.[1]

2. When do powers of representation come into effect?

A 2000 Act compliant POA can be one of three types: continuing (financial), welfare, or a combined continuing and welfare POA. For the POA to be used, it must be registered with the Office of the Public Guardian (Scotland) (OPG).[2]

Certain matters can impact the availability of powers under a registered POA:

- Welfare powers only become available when the granter loses capacity, or the attorney reasonably believes that the granter has lost capacity.[3] That is a matter that the courts, if necessary, can decide.[4] A solicitor is able to assess capacity. Given that a finding of incapacity would have legal consequences for the granter, it would be advisable for a doctor to carry out his or her own assessment.
- Continuing powers become available to attorneys immediately following registration of the POA with the OPG. However, a granter may include wording in the POA that suspends that until they become incapable.[5]
- The granter may instruct that the POA is not registered with the OPG until some later date. While that is permissible it may not be advisable.

3. Does your jurisdiction have a legal test for determining mental capacity?

Scotland has no legal definition of 'mental capacity'. Individuals aged 16 or older are presumed to have capacity unless there is evidence to the contrary.[6] The 2000 Act provides a definition of 'incapable':

> *'incapable' means incapable of –*
> *(a) acting; or*
> *(b) making decisions; or*
> *(c) communicating decisions; or*
> *(d) understanding decisions; or*
> *(e) retaining the memory of decisions, as mentioned in any provision of this Act, by reason of mental disorder or of inability to communicate because of physical disability; but a person shall not fall within this definition by reason only of a lack or deficiency in a faculty of communication if that lack or deficiency can be made good by human or mechanical aid (whether of an interpretative nature or otherwise).*[7]

4. Can the powers of representation deal with property and finances and/or health and welfare?

See the answer to question 2 above.

5. Are there any other protective measures available?

Yes, but regardless of the measure (POA or otherwise), general principles within the 2000 Act need to be observed, namely:

- the intervention must benefit the adult in a way that cannot be achieved without the intervention;[8]
- the intervention proposed will be the least restrictive and not unduly infringe on the adult's freedom;[9]
- in deciding if an intervention is required and what form it should take, due consideration should be given to:

  - the wishes and feelings of the adult concerned, so far as they can be determined by any means of communication;[10]
  - the views of the nearest relative, primary carer, any guardian or attorney, any person a sheriff[11] determines is to be consulted, and of anyone who has an interest in the adult or the intervention that is proposed (where those views have been made known);[12] and
- the adult who is to be the subject of the intervention must be encouraged to use the skills he or she has concerning his or her own affairs (property, financial affairs or personal welfare), and to develop new ones too.[13]

The main alternatives to a POA are an intervention or guardianship order, both being governed by the 2000 Act.[14]

An intervention order (IO) facilitates the making of 'one off' decisions for an adult because he or she lacks the capacity to do so (the Adult). Anyone claiming an interest in the personal welfare, property or financial affairs (the Affairs) of the Adult can apply to a sheriff to have an IO granted.[15] Care is advisable when applying for an IO as:

- it must be supported by certain reports in a specific form,[16] the detail of which will depend on the nature of the application, following examination of the Adult no more than 30 days before the lodging of the application with the Sheriff Court;[17]
- a sheriff needs to be satisfied that the Adult is incapable of managing his or her own Affairs and that the IO is appropriate in such circumstances; and
- it should only request sufficient authority to carry out the intended action.

Assuming the application is received favourably, a sheriff may direct specific action be taken, or authorise the party named in the order to take the relevant action.[18] IOs last only for as long as is necessary for the relevant act to be carried out,[19] and depending on its nature, will be notified to the relevant authority and subject to supervision.[20]

Guardianship orders (GOs) are useful when there is a need to provide ongoing care for an Adult – they can be financial or welfare oriented.[21] Anyone claiming an interest in the Affairs of the Adult can apply for a GO.[22] Applications for GOs must:

- be supported by a series of reports, following examination of the Adult no more than 30 days before the lodging of the application.[23] The nature of the reports required will depend on whether a financial or welfare GO is being sought but must be produced in a specific form;[24] and

- identify the powers being sought and satisfy the sheriff that the powers applied for are appropriate.

If an order is granted, the appointment will generally be for a period of three years though longer appointments are possible in some circumstances.[25] A sheriff may also determine that an IO would be more appropriate and grant that in place of a GO.

6. What are the formalities of establishing a power of representation?

So far as continuing POAs are concerned, the 2000 Act requires that:

- it is signed by the granter;[26]
- it contains a statement that the POA will be a continuing POA, even if the grantor loses capacity;[27]
- where it is intended only to be relied upon in the event of the grantor losing capacity, states that the granter has considered how incapacity is to be determined;[28] and
- it incorporates a certificate in the prescribed form by a practising solicitor, doctor or member of the Faculty of Advocates[29] that:
  - they interviewed the granter immediately before the granter signed the document;[30]
  - they are satisfied that, either owing to their own knowledge of the granter or because they have spoken with someone (named in the certificate) who has knowledge of the granter, that at the time the POA is being granted, the granter understands its nature and extent;[31] and
  - they have no reason to believe that the granter is acting under undue influence or that any other factor vitiates the granting of the power.[32]

The requirements for the purposes of granting a welfare POA are almost identical,[33] but the POA must include a statement that the granter has considered how his or her incapacity will be determined.[34]

7. Is there a registration process for powers of representation?

Yes, electronically or via a postal submission.[35] The time to register the POA under either facility depends on the number of registration requests that the OPG is dealing with at that time. Registrations can be expedited in certain circumstances.[36]

8. How can a power of representation be revoked or terminated (ie, in the event of marriage, divorce, death)?

A POA can be brought to an end in the following circumstances:

- by an express revocation by the granter. However, the granter

must retain capacity and the 'revocation notice' must comply with the 2000 Act and be communicated to the OPG;[37]
- where a sole attorney under a POA resigns and communicates that to the relevant authorities;[38]
- where the granter or a sole attorney dies;[39]
- where the granter of a POA appoints their spouse or civil partner to act as his or her attorney and he or she later, formally, terminates the relationship, except where the POA provides otherwise;[40]
- where there is later an application for guardianship made and granted, containing powers related to those which would have been available under the POA;[41]
- where a sheriff, following an application from someone claiming an interest in the Affairs of the granter of a POA and on cause shown, removes an attorney from office, or certain powers from an attorney;[42] and
- where an attorney exercising continuing powers is declared bankrupt, his or her powers to deal with financial matters ends.[43]

9. Is the process of making and/or registering a power of representation supervised by a court or government body?

It is the duty of the solicitor instructed to prepare the POA to satisfy him or herself that his or her client intends to grant a POA, understands the nature of doing so and has the requisite capacity to do so. It is the role of the OPG to register a POA when it is submitted for registration.[44]

10. Is there a governmental or administrative body with oversight of the validity of a power of representation and supervision of its use?

There is no active supervision of attorneys per se. Any concerns regarding the use of continuing powers should be raised with the OPG.[45] Concerns regarding the exercise of welfare powers should be raised with the local authority.[46]

11. What role do the courts in your jurisdiction have in relation to powers of representation?

The Sheriff Court can, in certain circumstances, direct that the attorney is subject to active supervision. Following an application by someone claiming an interest in the Affairs of the grantor of the POA,[47] and being satisfied that it is required to safeguard/promote the grantor's interests[48] the court may make any of the following orders:

- that a continuing attorney be supervised by the OPG;[49]
- that a continuing attorney submit accounts for audit to the OPG for any period;[50]
- that a welfare attorney be supervised by the local authority;[51]

- that a welfare attorney provide the sheriff with a report on his or her actions as welfare attorney for any period;[52]
- revoke the powers granted to an attorney under a continuing or welfare POA;[53] or
- revoke the attorney's appointment.[54]

12. Are foreign powers of representation legally recognised in your jurisdiction? If so, what is the applicable legal framework?

The OPG accepts that, under the 2000 Act, a foreign POA is automatically valid in Scotland.[55] However, there is no formal mechanism for having a foreign POA endorsed in Scots law. The OPG has available on its website a certificate that can be printed to accompany a foreign POA explaining that it is automatically valid in Scotland.[56]

13. Has your jurisdiction ratified The Hague Convention on the International Protection of Adults 2000? If not, are there any plans for your jurisdiction to do so in the near future?

The United Kingdom signed The Hague Convention on 1 April 2003, and it ratified the convention for Scotland, as one of the territorial units making up the United Kingdom, on 5 November 2003.[57] Section 85 of and Schedule 3 to the 2000 Act implement the convention under Scots law.

14. Is there any publicly available guidance on the law and procedure concerning powers of representation in your jurisdiction?

The OPG's website (www.publicguardian-scotland.gov.uk/) provides useful guidance, as does the Scottish government's code of practice for attorneys (www.gov.scot/publications/code-practice-continuing-welfare-attorneys-second-edition-updated-february-2018/).

Notes

1 POAs granted pre the 2000 Act can still, depending on their terms, be relied upon.
2 Adults with Incapacity (Scotland) Act 2000, Section 19(1).
3 *Ibid*, Section 16(5)(b).
4 *Richmond v Richmond* (1914) 111 LT 273.
5 Adults with Incapacity (Scotland) Act 2000, Section 15(3)(ba).
6 Age of Legal Capacity (Scotland) Act 1991, Section 1; see also *Lindsay v Watson* (1843) 5 D 1194; *AB v CB* (1937) SC 408, Lord Justice Clerk (Aitchison) at p418; *Re Sabatini* (1969) 114 SJ 35.
7 Adults with Incapacity (Scotland) Act 2000, Section 1(6).
8 *Ibid*, Section 1(2).
9 *Ibid*, Section 1(3).
10 *Ibid*, Section 1(4)(a). This covers both the present and past wishes.
11 In Scotland, most cases are held in a Sheriff Court, and the judge that hears those cases is known as a 'sheriff'. See Judiciary of Scotland, 'Sheriffs', https://judiciary.scot/home/judiciary/judicial-office-holders/sheriffs/sheriffs-1.
12 Adults with Incapacity (Scotland) Act 2000, Section 1(4)(b)–(d).
13 *Ibid*, Section 1(5).
14 There are other options available. It is best to take advice on what the most appropriate measure, in the circumstances, would be.
15 Adults with Incapacity (Scotland) Act 2000, Section 53(1).
16 See the Adults with Incapacity (Reports in Relation to Guardianship and Intervention Orders) (Scotland) Regulations 2002, www.legislation.gov.uk/ssi/2002/96/contents/made.

17 Adults with Incapacity (Scotland) Act 2000, Section 53(4).
18 *Ibid*, Sections 53(5)(a)–(b) and 56.
19 See OPG, "What is an intervention order?", www.publicguardian-scotland.gov.uk/intervention-orders.
20 Adults with Incapacity (Scotland) Act 2000, Section 53(10).
21 OPG, "What is a guardianship order?", www.publicguardian-scotland.gov.uk/guardianship-orders.
22 Adults with Incapacity (Scotland) Act 2000, Section 57(1).
23 *Ibid*, Section 57(3).
24 *Ibid*.
25 *Ibid*, Section 58(4).
26 *Ibid*, Section 15(3)(a).
27 *Ibid*, Section 15(3)(b).
28 *Ibid*, Section 15(3)(ba).
29 *Ibid*, Section 15(4).
30 *Ibid*, Section 15(3)(c)(i).
31 *Ibid*, Section 15(3)(c)(ii).
32 *Ibid*, Section 15(3)(c)(iii).
33 *Ibid*, Section 16(3)–(4).
34 *Ibid*, Section 16(3)(ba).
35 See OPG, "How to register your PoA", www.publicguardian-scotland.gov.uk/power-of-attorney/epoar/submitting-a-power-of-attorney.
36 *Ibid*.
37 Adults with Incapacity (Scotland) Act 2000, Section 22A.
38 *Ibid*, Section 23. Note that a resignation only takes effect after the passage of a prescribed period of time.
39 See OPG, "Circumstances that bring a PoA to an end", www.publicguardian-scotland.gov.uk/power-of-attorney/registration/ending-a-power-of-attorney#:~:text=The%20PoA%20will%20end%20when,is%20no%20substitute%20attorney%20appointed.
40 Adults with Incapacity (Scotland) Act 2000, Section 24(1)–(1A).
41 *Ibid*, Section 24(2).
42 *Ibid*, Section 20(1) and (2)(e).
43 *Ibid*, Section 15(5). This will also be the result if the granter of the POA is declared bankrupt.
44 OPG, "Our role", www.publicguardian-scotland.gov.uk/power-of-attorney/power-of-attorney/our-role.
45 Adults with Incapacity (Scotland) Act 2000, Section 6(2)(c).
46 *Ibid*, Section 10(1)(c)(i).
47 *Ibid*, Section 20(1).
48 *Ibid*, Section 20(2).
49 *Ibid*, Section 20(2)(a).
50 *Ibid*, Section 20(2)(b).
51 *Ibid*, Section 20(2)(c).
52 *Ibid*, Section 20(2)(d).
53 *Ibid*, Section 20(2)(e)(i).
54 *Ibid*, Section 20(2)(e)(ii).
55 OPG, "FAQs – Can a non-Scottish PoA be used in Scotland?", www.publicguardian-scotland.gov.uk/power-of-attorney/faqs.
56 *Ibid*.
57 See Hague Conference on Private International Law – Conférence de La Haye de droit international privé, "*Protection of Adults Convention to receive its first ratification*" (13 November 2003), www.hcch.net/en/news-archive/details/?varevent=84.

Singapore

Yue-En Chong
Bethel Chambers LLC

1. Does your jurisdiction have legislation providing for powers of representation such as ordinary, continuing, enduring or lasting powers of attorney?

Yes – Section 11 of the Mental Capacity Act 2008 (MCA 2008). Unless stated otherwise, all the sections referred to in this chapter are sections of the MCA 2008. Also, it would be interesting to point out at this juncture that the MCA 2008 is *pari materia* in many parts with the England and Wales Mental Capacity Act 2005 as it was the choice of the Singapore government to model Singapore's MCA 2008 on this.

In essence, a lasting power of attorney (LPA) is a legal document and a deed where a donor appoints a donee to manage the donor's affairs and make decisions for and on behalf of the donor in the event the donor loses his or her mental capacity.

An ordinary power of attorney can be made in Singapore under Part 10 of the Conveyancing and Law of Property Act 1886 (CLPA 1886). Unless the power of attorney was made to be irrevocable for a fixed time,[1] the power of attorney is revoked by intervening events such as the death, marriage, mental disorder or bankruptcy of the donor.

2. When do powers of representation come into effect?

An LPA is created when it is registered with the Office of the Public

Guardian in accordance with the First Schedule of the MCA 2008 before 14 November 2022, which is the commencement of the Mental Capacity (Amendment) Act 2021. After 14 November 2022 there is an additional requirement that an LPA is made using the Office of the Public Guardian Online transaction system, called 'OPGO'.[2] However, a donee may only make decisions under an LPA where P (the person lacking capacity) lacks capacity, or the donee reasonably believes that P lacks capacity.[3] A certificate from a registered medical practitioner stating that P's lack of capacity is likely to be permanent can be requested by a person dealing with a donee.[4]

3. Does your jurisdiction have a legal test for determining mental capacity?

Yes, the MCA 2008 sets out that a person lacks capacity in relation to a matter if at the material time the person is unable to make a decision for him or herself in relation to a matter because of an impairment of, or a disturbance in, the functioning of the brain.[5] It does not matter whether this impairment is permanent or temporary.[6]

It would be observed that any question of whether a person lacks capacity would be a question of fact and decided on a balance of probabilities.[7]

However, the MCA 2008 does set forth a series of guiding principles and values that help in determining mental capacity. For example, it cautions about establishing incapacity simply on a person's age or appearance or a condition or an aspect of a person's behaviour which might lead others to make unjustified assumptions about the person's capacity.[8] Inherent in this espoused value is caution against ageism and prejudice against the physical appearance of an individual in determining that the person lacks capacity.

Additionally, the MCA 2008[9] sets out five core principles that must be applied to determine whether a person lacks mental capacity, namely that:

- there is a presumption that the person has capacity unless it is established that he or she lacks capacity;
- a person is not to be treated as unable to make a decision unless all practicable steps to help him or her do so have been taken without success;
- a person is not to be treated as unable to make a decision merely because he or she makes an unwise decision;
- an act done, or a decision made, on behalf of a person who lacks capacity must be done or made in his or her best interests; and
- when acting or making a decision on behalf of a person who lacks capacity, the action or decision taken should be less restrictive on that person's right and freedom to act.

To determine if a person is 'unable to make a decision', could be because of the failure of any one of the following four factors, that is, the ability to:

- understand the information relevant to the decision;
- retain that information;
- use or weigh that information as part of the process of making the decision; or
- communicate his or her decision (whether by talking, using sign language or any other means).[10]

Crucially, the information relevant to a decision includes information about the reasonably foreseeable consequences of deciding one way or another or failing to make a decision.[11]

Guidance is once again given as what concerns the mental capacity test is the ability of the person to make a decision in a 'material time', insofar that the person does retain the information relevant to a decision for a short period only does not prevent the person from being regarded as unable to make a decision.[12]

Emphasis is placed on ensuring that a person is only regarded as being unable to understand the information relevant to his or her decision after still failing to understand the information after it was explained to him or her in a way that is appropriate for his or her circumstances (ie, though the use of simple language, visual aids, language that they are most familiar with or any other means).[13]

4. Can the powers of representation deal with property and finances and/or health and welfare?

An LPA[14] is a legal document that allows a person (donor) to appoint another (donee) to act and make decisions on their behalf in matters concerning the donor's personal welfare, including healthcare matters, or property and affairs, including financial matters, or both in the event the donor is assessed to lack mental capacity to act or make such decisions for him or herself.

An LPA takes effect only when the donor is found to lack mental capacity as under Section 4(1).

5. Are there any other protective measures available?

Having an LPA is crucial to futureproofing a donor's personal and financial affairs and is highly recommended by the Ministry of Social and Family Development as a protective measure against any untoward happenstance. It safeguards a donor's interests and well-being in the event he or she lacks mental capacity. The donor has a choice of appointing a single donee or multiple donees, acting jointly and severally, to act and make decisions on behalf of the donor.

In the event the donor does not have a suitable next-of-kin or close friend to appoint as a donee, the donor may appoint a registered professional as his or her professional donee.

In the event that the donor does not have suitable family members or friends to appoint as his or her donee(s), the donor may choose to appoint a professional donee[15] to act in the best interests of the donor. A professional donee consists of professionals from selected professional groups, such as lawyers, doctors, healthcare professionals and social workers, to name a few, who meet the qualifying criteria, pass a certification course and who are registered with the Office of the Public Guardian. Safeguards are in place to ensure that professional deputies fulfil and maintain high standards of discipline and professionalism in acting in the best interests of the donor.

In the event that an LPA has not been executed, the Family Justice Courts[16] can appoint a deputy (ie, an adult guardian) to be given powers to make decisions for the person lacking capacity's personal welfare and properties and affairs. The Family Justice Courts can also directly make orders or a decision for the person lacking capacity and this is considered preferable to the appointment of a deputy.[17] There are two avenues for deputyship application – simplified and standard.[18]

6. What are the formalities of establishing a power of representation?

The formalities for the creation of an LPA can be found in the First Schedule of the MCA 2008. It must be executed before a witness, called a 'certificate issuer', who states that the donor understands the purpose of the instrument and the scope of the authority conferred under it, that no fraud or undue pressure is being used to induce the donor to create an LPA and that there is nothing else which would prevent an LPA from being created by the instrument. The donor must be at least 21 years of age and have the mental capacity to create the LPA.[19]

The donee and/or replacement donee must be at least 21 years of age. In the matter of making decisions relating to the donor's personal welfare, the donee must be an individual and, in the matter of making decisions relating to the donor's property and affairs, the donee may be an individual (but must not be a bankrupt) or a licensed trust company as defined in the Trust Companies Act.[20]

In the event the donor does not have a suitable next-of-kin or close friend to appoint as a donee, the donor may appoint a registered professional as his or her professional donee.[21]

7. Is there a registration process for powers of representation?

To ensure the enforceability of the LPA, it is mandatory to register it with the Singapore Office of the Public Guardian (OPG).

All submissions of the LPA for registration must be done electronically via the OPG Online system (OPGO) using Singpass. The donor fills out the online LPA form with details and powers to be granted to the donee after which the nominated donee will need to log onto OPGO with their Singpass and accept the appointment. The donor is then required to get the LPA form certified by a certified issuer.[22]

A 'Certified Issuer' refers to:[23]

- a legally qualified medical practitioner who is registered as a specialist in psychiatry under the Medical Registration Act 1997;
- a legally qualified medical practitioner who is accredited by the Public Guardian to issue LPA Certificates; or
- an advocate and solicitor of the Supreme Court who has in force a practising certificate under the Legal Professional Act 1966.

The waiting period before an LPA is registered is three weeks. The OPG will register the LPA at the end of three weeks if there are no objections.

Hardcopy LPAs will only be accepted in exceptional circumstances.[24]

8. How can a power of representation be revoked or terminated (ie, in the event of marriage, divorce or death)?

An LPA will be automatically revoked or terminated:[25]

- by the donor at any time while the donor still has capacity to do so;
- upon the death of the donor or the donee (in the case of only one donee and there is no replacement donee(s));
- where the donor or donee becomes bankrupt, in which case this only revokes the LPA insofar as it relates to the donor's property and affairs, however, the LPA is still effective with regards to the donor's personal welfare;
- in the event the donee is a corporation, upon the liquidation, winding up, dissolution of the donee or when the corporation is placed under judicial management;
- upon dissolution or annulment of a marriage between the donor and the donee unless the LPA states otherwise; or
- where the donee loses mental capacity.

In such scenarios as those set out above, every donee and the OPG must be informed of the revocation.

9. Is the process of making and/or registering a power of representation supervised by a court or government body?

The LPA in Singapore is governed by the Mental Capacity Act 2008.

To ensure the enforceability of the LPA, it is mandatory to register it with the OPG. The registration provides supervision and protection of the donor's interests as well as an avenue for third parties to verify the validity and authority of the donee(s).

While not mandatory, in the case of LPA Form 1, it is highly recommended to seek legal advice when making an LPA so that the document accurately reflects the donor's intentions and meets all legal requirements. In the event the donor wishes to impose conditions and restrictions on the donee, he or she can do so by using LPA Form 2, in which case a lawyer must be engaged to draft such conditions and restrictions.

10. Is there a governmental or administrative body with oversight of the validity of a power of representation and supervision of its use?

The OPG provides supervision and protection of the donor's interests as well as an avenue for third parties to verify the validity and authority of the donee(s).

The OPG carries out functions to enable and protect persons who lack mental capacity.[26]

11. What role do the courts in your jurisdiction have in relation to powers of representation?

The Singapore courts have powers over two main areas, the first is in relation to the validity of the LPA[27] and the second is in relation to the operation of the LPA.[28]

In determining the validity of the LPA, the court may determine if the formalities required for the creation of the LPA have been met and if this has not been met, may direct that the LPA is not to be registered.

Should the court determine that fraud or undue pressure was used to induce P to create an LPA,[29] or that the donee has been convicted of certain criminal offences or engages or proposes to engage in conduct that would contravene the donee's authority, and not in P's best interest, the court can revoke the LPA.[30]

12. Are foreign powers of representation legally recognised in your jurisdiction? If so, what is the applicable legal framework?

While foreign instruments similar to a Singapore LPA are not directly enforceable under Singapore law, they can be taken into account by the Singapore courts when considering whether to vest such Singapore assets in the donee.

Paragraph 7 of the Second Schedule to the Mental Capacity Act 2008 prescribes as follows:

> *(1) Sub-paragraph (2) applies if the court is satisfied –*
> *(a) that* ***under the law prevailing in a place outside Singapore a person ('M') has been appointed to exercise powers in respect of the property or affairs of P on the ground (however formulated) that P lacks capacity to make decisions with respect to the management and administration of P's property and affairs****; and*
> *(b) that, having regard to the nature of the appointment and to the circumstances of the case, it is* ***expedient*** *that the court should exercise its powers under this paragraph.*
>
> *(2) The court may direct –*
> *(a) any property situated in Singapore standing in the name of P; or*
> *(b) any stocks standing in the name of P or the right to receive dividends from such stocks,* ***to be transferred into M's name or otherwise dealt with as required by M****, and may give such directions as the court thinks fit for dealing with accrued dividends from the stocks* [**emphasis added**].

Where an application under paragraph 7 is successful, the applicant is not appointed as a deputy for P but rather P's assets in Singapore are vested in the applicant and, instead of the applicant being under the supervision of the OPG, the applicant would remain subject to the laws of where the foreign instrument similar to a Singapore LPA was created.

It is important to highlight that the requirements under paragraph 7(1)(b), as extracted above, is the critical test in convincing the Singapore court to grant such an application.[31]

13. Has your jurisdiction ratified The Hague Convention on the International Protection of Adults 2000? If not, are there any plans for your jurisdiction to do so in the near future?

No, and there are currently no plans to rectify it. The reason cited is because of the difference in the formal requirements to make an LPA from country to country and that it is in Singapore's interest to ensure that robust safeguards are in place to ensure that the interests of the donor are protected.[32]

14. Is there any publicly available guidance on the law and procedure concerning powers of representation in your jurisdiction?

There is publicly accessible guidance on the law and procedures concerning an LPA. The Office of Public Guardian (OPG) website,[33] for example, provides the public with a robust explanation on the benefits of drawing up an LPA and a step-by-step guide on how to create and register an LPA with the OPG. An infographic is also provided on the OPG website detailing what needs to be done.

Notes

1 Conveyancing and Law of Property Act 1886, Section 44.
2 Mental Capacity Act 2008, Section 11(2)(b)(i) and 11(2)(b)(ii).
3 Mental Capacity Act 2008, Section 13(1).
4 Mental Capacity Act 2008, Section 13(10).
5 Mental Capacity Act 2008, Section 4(1).
6 *Ibid*, Section 4(2).
7 *Ibid*, Section 4(4).
8 *Ibid*, Section 4(3).
9 *Ibid*, Section 3.
10 *Ibid*, Section 5(1).
11 *Ibid*, Section 5(4).
12 *Ibid*, Section 5(3).
13 *Ibid*, Section 5(2).
14 *Ibid*, Section 11(1).
15 *Ibid*, Section 12(1)(a)(ii) and (iii).
16 *Ibid*, Section 19.
17 *Ibid*, Section 20(4)(a).
18 See www.judiciary.gov.sg/family/before-applying-to-be-deputy.
19 Mental Capacity Act 2008, Section 11 and OPG, *A Guide to: The Lasting Power of Attorney*, www.msf.gov.sg/docs/default-source/opg/lpa_guide_english.pdf.
20 *Ibid*.
21 OPG, *A Guide to: The Lasting Power of Attorney*, Part C, www.msf.gov.sg/docs/default-source/opg/lpa_guide_english.pdf.
22 See OPG, "How to Make a Lasting Power of Attorney", www.msf.gov.sg/what-we-do/opg/lasting-power-of-attorney/how-to-make-a-lasting-power-of-attorney.
23 Mental Capacity Regulations 2010, Rule 7.
24 Mental Capacity Act 2008, Section 11(2A); paragraph 1.2 of the *Lasting Power of Attorney Certificate Issuer Guide*, www.msf.gov.sg/docs/default-source/opg/lpa_certificate_issuer_guide.pdf.
25 *Ibid*, Section 15.
26 *Ibid*, Section 31.
27 *Ibid*, Section 17.
28 *Ibid*, Section 18.
29 *Ibid*, Section 18(3)(a).
30 *Ibid*, Section 18(4)(a) and (b).
31 See *Law Gazette*, "Foreign LPAs: Recognition, Enforceability and Practical Issues", https://lawgazette.com.sg/practice/practice-matters/foreign-lpas-recognition-enforceability-and-practical-issues/.
32 See MSF, "Data on Cases of Conflicts Between a Singapore Lasting Power of Attorney (LPA) and a Foreign LPA Executed by the Same Donor", www.msf.gov.sg/media-room/article/Data-on-Cases-of-Conflicts-Between-a-Singapore-Lasting-Power-of-Attorney-LPA-and-a-Foreign-LPA-Executed-by-the-Same-Donor.
33 OPG, www.msf.gov.sg/what-we-do/opg/home.

United States: Financial powers of representation

Shelley Rhoads Perry
Senior Advocacy Group

The United States is made up of 50 states, the District of Columbia, Puerto Rico and the United States Virgin Islands. Each jurisdiction enacts its own laws which govern all powers of representation of individuals. The US powers of representation include financial and medical powers of attorney (POA). The two areas are governed by different state statutes, and the trend is to include language in the financial power of attorney which makes it clear to the agent and third parties that medical decisions are the responsibility of the health care agent.

The Uniform Law Commission (ULC) incorporated the first uniform POA in the Uniform Probate Code in 1969. ULC published its first Uniform Power of Attorney Act in 1979. There was a 1988 revision and another revision in 2006. The 2006 revision (UPOAA) is the most current act. Thirty-two states have enacted the UPOAA.

This chapter presents answers based on the UPOAA, but details where California,[1] New York[2] and Florida[3] statutes agree or diverge from the Uniform Act. The states of California, New York and Florida were chosen because they have not enacted the UPOAA, and have a significant elder population.

1. Does your jurisdiction have legislation providing for power of representation such as ordinary, continuing, enduring or lasting powers of attorney?

In the United States, a power of representation is referred to as a POA. A principal is the person executing the POA who gives authority to an individual called an agent or attorney-in-fact.

A POA can be used to delegate legal authority to another person for both financial and medical matters. A medical POA is most often included in an Advance Healthcare Directive. The financial and medical POAs are governed by different statutes in most jurisdictions, and there is limited overlap in powers. (See the chapter entitled "United States: Health care powers of representation".)

The types of POAs recognised in the United States are:

- general: gives broad unrestricted powers;
- durable: takes effect when executed and is not terminated by the principal's incapacity;
- non-durable: takes effect when executed and terminates if the principal becomes incapacitated;
- springing: takes effect upon the happening of a specific future event, usually the principal's incapacity; and
- limited: gives authority to conduct a specific act, ie, sell real property.

The UPOAA creates a durable POA effective immediately, unless expressly stated otherwise.[4] The Florida legislature enacted a new POA statute in October 2011 which created a default durable POA (general or limited), and substantially invalidated springing POAs which are contingent on the principal's incapacity. There are some exceptions to the springing POA ban for foreign POAs and those executed before 1 October 2011.[5] New York and California recognise durable, non-durable, limited and springing POAs, but the statutory short form POAs default to durable.

2. When do powers of representation come into effect?

The UPOAA default is that the POA is exercisable when executed.[6] However, the principal may make the effective date contingent on a future event (most often incapacity) if it explicitly states the contingency in the document. Florida's default effective date is when executed by the principal.[7] California's statutory short form POA states that it is a general durable POA that becomes effective only upon the principal's disability or incapacity.[8] New York's statutory short POA has a 'modifications' section where the principal can make additional provisions overriding the default effective date.[9] In New York and California, the effective date is the date executed by the agent, not the principal.

3. Does your jurisdiction have a legal test for determining mental capacity?

The mental capacity standard required to execute a POA can vary depending on the jurisdiction and the type of POA being considered. In general, the principal must have the mental capacity to understand the nature and effect of the document being signed.

This usually means that the principal must understand:

- the purpose and scope of the power of attorney;
- the powers being granted to the agent;
- the consequences of granting these powers; and
- the nature and extent of the principal's property and affairs.

The capacity required doesn't necessarily require the same level of understanding needed to create a will.

Capacity evaluation is required if the principal executed a springing POA which will become effective when the principal is deemed incapacitated. The UPOAA allows for the principal to authorise a certain person to make the capacity assessment.[10] If the principal is deemed incapacitated, that person may also act as the principal's representative pursuant to federal HIPAA regulations[11] which authorises access to the principal's health records and medical providers.

If no such person is named or available, the UPOAA outlines a process to establish the incapacity of the principal.[12] The UPOAA defines incapacity as the "inability of an individual to manage property or business affairs because the individual has an impairment in the ability to receive and evaluate information or make or communicate decisions even with the use of technological assistance".[13] In order to establish the mental incapacity of the principal, a physician or licensed psychologist must state in writing that the principal is incapacitated as per this definition.

To determine incapacity under the Florida POA statute, an affidavit must be executed by a physician who has primary responsibility for the treatment and care of the principal, who is licensed to practise medicine in the jurisdiction, and who will state in the affidavit a belief that the principal lacks the capacity to manage property.[14]

California's process in its statutory short form POA is similar to the UPOAA, and also allows the principal to name an individual to determine incapacity.[15] If a physician's examination is required, it must take place later than the date of the POA's execution, and must certify in writing that the principal is incapable of managing financial affairs.

New York's statutory short form POA does not define any process for establishing incapacity, but the POA statute contains a definition for incapacity.[16]

4. Can the power of representation deal with property and finances and/or health and welfare?

The UPOAA only deals with property and financial transactions. The UPOAA, California, Florida and New York statutory short form POAs state that the POA does not authorise the agent to make health care decisions.[17] However, Florida allows the agent to make health care decisions on behalf of the principal if specifically authorised in the POA.[18]

The ULC has issued a Uniform Act specifically for health and welfare, the Uniform Health-Care Decisions Act 2023. It is in the early stages of roll-out to the states. Florida health and welfare powers are governed by Chapter 765. In California, Advance Medical Directives which deal with health and welfare are governed by Sections 4670–4806 of the California Probate Code. In New York, Chapter 45, Section 4306A deals with Advance Medical Directives. Advance Medical Directives include the naming of a health care agent (usually called a 'surrogate' or 'proxy'), instructions by the principal about medical care and a living will that gives directions to physicians if the principal is determined to have a terminal condition. (See the chapter entitled "United States: Health care powers of representation".)

5. Are there any other protective measures available?

The only protective measure available to principals if they fail to execute a POA or if the POA itself fails for some reason is a guardianship of the property.[19] The UPOAA statutory form includes an optional section where the principal can name an individual who would be considered first choice for guardian.[20] Florida has a pre-need guardian provision[21] in its guardianship statutes, and a separate document can be executed and filed with the court at the same time the POA is executed.

6. What are the formalities of establishing a power of representation?

The UPOAA has minimal execution formalities, leaving more specific direction to each state. In all jurisdictions, the POA must be in writing; the agent and principal must both be over 18 years of age; and they both must have mental capacity, meaning an understanding of the contents of the document being signed. Under the UPOAA, either a witness or a notary is required to sign, and the principal must sign or someone in the principal's 'conscious presence' may sign.[22]

In New York, the POA must be signed by the principal (or a principal's representative) and two subscribing witnesses and be acknowledged by a notary public. The notary public may also be a witness. If the principal is unable to sign, the notary may sign the principal's name on the power of attorney. The agent must also sign in front of a notary and two subscribing witnesses. There is also a requirement for a POA to have 'substantially conforming' language to the statutory short form POA.[23]

In California, the principal may choose to sign in front of two subscribing witnesses or a notary public. The agent must also sign with the same formalities. California also has a requirement that notices and warnings on the statutory short form POA must be included in a non-statutory POA. Clear statements declaring it a durable or springing POA also must be included.[24]

In all states, the agent must not be a witness or the notary public. Florida, New York and California have all enacted some form of remote online notary (RON), although New York specifically excludes RON for POAs. In Florida, the notary block must contain the statement electing "physical presence or online presence" to be valid.

7. Is there a registration process for powers of representation?

The UPOAA is silent on this topic, and there is no legal requirement for a POA to be registered.[25] However, the principal or principal's attorney may record the POA with the appropriate Clerk of Courts to make it part of the official record. The principal would be able to obtain certified copies of the POA which could assist with its acceptance by third parties. A revocation of the POA would also need to be recorded. Some legal practitioners will 'escrow' the POA, meaning keep it in the attorney's document vault, and make available to the appointed agent only upon the principal's incapacity.

8. How can a power of representation be revoked or terminated (ie, in the event of marriage, divorce or death)?

Under the UPOAA and all states, a durable POA automatically terminates upon the death of the principal. A POA will also terminate if:

- the principal becomes incapacitated and the POA is not durable;
- it was a limited POA for a special purpose (like the transfer of real estate), and the purpose was accomplished;
- the date of termination was specified in the document and is reached;
- the agent dies, becomes incapacitated, resigns or is otherwise unavailable, and there is no alternate agent named;
- upon the filing of an action to dissolve or annul the agent's marriage to the principal (if the POA does not otherwise provide);

- the principal is adjudicated incapacitated, and the court chooses not to keep the POA in place;[26] or
- the principal revokes the POA.

The principal may revoke a POA by expressly stating the revocation in a subsequent POA or other writing signed by the principal. If the revocation is not expressly stated, the previous POA is still in effect.[27]

9. Is the process of making and/or registering a power of representation supervised by a court or government body?

The process of making and executing POAs is not typically supervised by a court or government body in any jurisdiction. The original intent of the UPOAA was to offer a low-cost, private method for those with modest assets to plan for incapacity instead of being subjected to the more expensive and restrictive court-supervised guardianship process.[28] California, Florida and New York also do not require court supervision or registration.

10. Is there a governmental or administrative body with oversight of the validity of a power of representation and supervision of its use?

Beyond the court system, there is no specific governmental or administrative body with oversight of the validity of a POA or supervision of its use. However, in California, professional fiduciaries who serve as agents are regulated by the Department of Consumer Affairs Professional Fiduciaries Bureau, and may be supervised when acting as POAs.[29]

11. What role do the courts in your jurisdiction have in relation to powers of representation?

Most jurisdictions have enacted judicial relief and conflicts of interest provisions in the states' POA statutes. The UPOAA views judicial relief as a way to protect vulnerable or incapacitated adults.[30] It delineates who may petition a court to construe or enforce a POA, review the agent's actions and grant appropriate relief.[31] The list of potential petitioners are similar in Florida, California and New York. The following persons may petition the court:

- the principal or the agent, including any nominated successor agent;
- a guardian, conservator, trustee or other fiduciary acting for the principal;
- a person authorised to make health care decisions for the principal;
- the principal's spouse, parent or descendant;
- an individual who would qualify as the presumptive heir of the principal;

- a person named as a beneficiary to receive any property, benefit or contractual right on the principal's death or as a beneficiary of a trust created by or for the principal that has a financial interest in the principal's estate;
- a governmental agency having regulatory authority to protect the welfare of the principal;
- the principal's caregiver or another person that demonstrates sufficient interest in the principal's welfare; and
- a person asked to accept the power of attorney.

12. Are foreign powers of representation legally recognised in your jurisdiction? If so, what is the applicable legal framework?

Portability is a major issue in all jurisdictions. The general rule under the UPOAA and most jurisdictions validates a POA executed in one state if its execution complied with the laws of that state at the time of execution. Non-US POAs are not specifically recognised under the UPOAA.

Recent UPOAA and state legislative amendments have attempted to make it easier for a foreign POA to be accepted by third parties (primarily financial institutions) regardless of jurisdiction of execution or implementation. They have enacted specific language providing a path to validation of a foreign POA to encourage acceptance by third parties,[32] but have also included language that establishes statutory liability for third parties who unreasonably refuse an acknowledged POA.[33]

Florida has a similar provision and adds language protecting third parties if they reject the foreign POA.[34] The foreign POA will be valid, but the agent may act only as authorised by Florida law and the terms of the POA. The third party may request an opinion of counsel from the other state or an affidavit stating it was executed in conformance with that state's laws.[35] Florida does not specifically recognise non-US POAs, but implies acceptance if the non-US POA was executed with Florida-mandated requirements.

In California, a POA executed in another state or jurisdiction which is in compliance with the law of that state (or California's) at the time of execution is valid and enforceable to the same extent as a California POA, whether or not the principal is domiciled in California.[36]

New York also recognises out-of-state and non-US POAs if executed with the formalities required at the time and place of execution, with some exceptions and limitations.[37]

Challenges using foreign POAs and their acceptance by third parties are outside the scope of this chapter.

13. Has your jurisdiction ratified The Hague Convention on the International Protection of Adults 2000? If not, are there any plans for your jurisdiction to do so in the near future?

The Hague Convention on the International Protection of Adults 2000 would be ratified at the federal level and POAs are governed by state law.

14. Is there any publicly available guidance on the law and procedure concerning powers of representation in your jurisdiction?

There is widespread free information available from public sources on POAs. The UPOAA publishes a statutory form and agent certification on its website for use by attorneys and lay people.[38] The form follows the default provisions of the UPOAA, but is adaptable to multiple jurisdictional legislation. Florida,[39] California[40] and New York[41] all provide statutory short forms as part of the specific state legislation available online. The State Bar Associations and public libraries also offer consumer information on the uses of a POA, and where to download statutory forms.

Notes

1 Cal Prob Code § 4000-4545.
2 NY GOL § 5-1501-5-1514.
3 Fla Stat § 709.
4 Uniform Power of Attorney Act 2006, Section 104.
5 A Florida POA executed after 1 October 2011 which is to become effective at a future date or upon a future event is ineffective, unless it is a military power of attorney.
6 Uniform Power of Attorney Act 2006, Section 109(a).
7 Fla Stat § 709.2108(1).
8 Cal Prob Code § 4401.
9 NY GOL § 5-1513.
10 Uniform Power of Attorney Act 2006, Section 109(b).
11 Health Insurance Portability and Accountability Act, Sections 1171–1179 of the Social Security Act 42 USC Section 1320d.
12 Uniform Power of Attorney Act 2006, Section 109(c).
13 *Ibid*, Section 102(5)(A).
14 Fla Sta. § 709.2108 (2).
15 Cal Prob Code § 4405(a).
16 NY GOL § 5-1501(2)(c).
17 See Uniform Power of Attorney Act 2006, Section 301 – 'important information'.
18 Fla Stat § 709.2201(2)(c).
19 As opposed to a plenary guardian which is guardian of person and property.
20 Uniform Power of Attorney Act 2006, Section 103.
21 Fla St § 744.3045.
22 See Uniform Power of Attorney Act 2006, Section 105 – 'comments'.
23 NY GOL § 5-1501(2)(n)(ii).
24 Cal Prob Code § 4124.
25 With the exception of a real estate POA, which must be recorded as part of the transaction.
26 In California and New York, the divorce or annulment must be by final decree, not just filed.
27 Uniform Power of Attorney Act 2006, Section 110(f).
28 See *ibid* – 'summary'.
29 See www.fiduciary.ca.gov/about_us/.
30 See Uniform Power of Attorney Act 2006, Section 116 – 'comment'.
31 *Ibid*, Section 116(a)(1)–(9).
32 *Ibid*, Section 119.
33 *Ibid*, Section 120.
34 Fla St § 709.2106(3).
35 See www.floridabar.org, consumer pamphlet 13.
36 Cal Prob Code § 4053.
37 NY GOL § 5-1501.

38 Uniform Power of Attorney Act 2006, Section 301.
39 Fla St § 709.2105.
40 Cal Prob Code.
41 NY GOL § 5-1513.

United States: Health care powers of representation

Shelley Rhoads Perry
Senior Advocacy Group

The Uniform Law Commission (ULC) has issued a Uniform Act specifically for health and welfare, the Health-Care Decisions Act (2023). It is in the early stages of roll-out to the states, but is new enough to incorporate the most recent ideas and legislation introduced or enacted across the United States. Advance Health-Care Directive legislation is a fast-evolving area of state law. This chapter follows the ULC Health-Care Decisions Act 2023 (UHCDA).

1. Does your jurisdiction have legislation providing for power of representation such as ordinary, continuing, enduring or lasting powers of attorney?

Under the UHCDA, and in most states, powers of representation are often included in an Advance Health-Care Directive (AHCD) (also known as an Advance Medical Directive).[1] The AHCD includes the naming of a health care agent (usually called a 'surrogate' or 'proxy'), instructions by the principal about medical care, and a living will which gives directions to physicians if the principal is determined to have a terminal condition.

The health care surrogate (HCS) authority is most often a durable springing power of attorney. It is not invalidated by the principal's incapacity, and is, by default, only effective upon the principal's incapacity. Unlike the financial power of attorney (POA) agent, the

AHCD not only grants authority, but also gives specific instructions on the actions the HCS must take on behalf of the principal.

2. When do powers of representation come into effect?

Unless specified otherwise in the document, the HCS becomes effective when the principal is deemed incapacitated. The principal may include a provision in the document to make the appointment effective immediately if he or she needs assistance accessing medical records or filing insurance claims, although he or she still has health care decision-making control.

3. Does your jurisdiction have a legal test for determining mental capacity?

The UHCDA determines the mental capacity test as: "willing and able to communicate a decision independently or with appropriate services, technological assistance, supported decision making, or some reasonable accommodation".[2]

The capacity test becomes more specific depending upon the action. There is a different test for the making or revoking of a health care decision and instruction, and the appointment of a health care surrogate.

In order to revoke a health care decision or instruction, the principal must understand the nature and consequences of the decision or instruction, including the risks and benefits.[3]

The principal's capacity evaluation is required to make the HCS powers effective. The capacity test for appointing an HCS is the principal recognises the identity of the individual being appointed and understands the general nature of the relationship between them.[4]

There is a presumption of capacity when an individual is being evaluated to determine health care decision-making ability. The presumption may be rebutted by a court determination of incapacity or a contemporaneous examination by a physician, psychologist or other individual with training and expertise in the finding of lack of capacity who is authorised to practise in the jurisdiction.[5]

The UHCDA includes several provisions outlining a process to object to a finding of the principal's incapacity which do not require court intervention.[6]

4. Can the power of representation deal with property and finances and/or health and welfare?

The AHCD and HCS appointment only authorises a power of attorney for health care.

5. Are there any other protective measures available?

There is a recognition among members of the state legislatures and health care communities that many people do not execute an AHCD or appoint an HCS. Given this reality, the UHCDA included provisions for a default surrogate which allows family members and other people close to the patient to make decisions in the event the patient lacks capacity and has not appointed an HCS.[7]

As with financial POAs, a court-appointed guardian is the primary protective measure available when no HCS has been appointed or if the appointment is invalid for some reason. In this case it would be a guardian of the person. A principal may name a pre-need guardian in an AHCD, financial POA, or separate writing which names a plenary guardian.[8]

6. What are the formalities of establishing a power of representation?

Under the UHCDA, the formalities of establishing an AHCD are less stringent than those for establishing a financial POA. The minimum requirements call for one witness to be present, either physically or electronically,[9] when the principal signs the document. A notary is not a requirement. Since an HCS has life and death decision making over the principal, the UHCDA includes a long list of individuals who *cannot* be an HCS or a witness.[10]

7. Is there a registration process for powers of representation?

There is a trend in many states to set up a state-wide advance directive database where principals can register their AHCDs.[11] Theoretically, the ACHDs would then be available to medical providers if the principal becomes incapacitated. Most medical providers request individuals to provide an AHCD and/or complete a proprietary form at an appointment.

8. How can a power of representation be revoked or terminated (ie, marriage, divorce or death)?

Under the UHCDA and all states, an AHCD and HCS appointment automatically terminates upon the death of the principal. A principal may revoke an AHCD and/or HCS provided the principal has not been deemed incapacitated by a physician or the court.[12] The HCS appointment may be revoked by an oral statement to a health care professional.[13] The HCS is revoked automatically (unless stated otherwise in the AHCD) if:

- a petition or decree for annulment, divorce, dissolution of marriage, legal separation or termination has been filed and not dismissed or withdrawn;
- the principal and spouse have agreed in writing to a legal separation; or

- the spouse has abandoned the principal for more than one year.[14]

9. Is the process of making and/or registering a power of representation supervised by a court or government body?
The process of making and executing an AHCD is not typically supervised by a court or government body in any jurisdiction.

10. Is there a governmental or administrative body with oversight of the validity of a power of representation and supervision of its use?
Beyond a petition to the court, there is no specific governmental or administrative body with oversight of the validity of an AHCD or the supervision of its use.

11. What role do the courts in your jurisdiction have in relation to powers of representation?
Under the UHCDA, separate sections contain provisions for Judicial Review of Finding of a Lack of Capacity and Judicial Relief. The courts may be brought in on two issues: when there is a question as to whether the principal has capacity,[15] and when the agent's actions might not be in line with the provisions of the AHCD.[16]

12. Are foreign powers of representation legally recognised in your jurisdiction? If so, what is the applicable legal framework?
An AHCD and HCS appointment is valid across states if it was executed correctly under the state law specified in the AHCD or the state in which the principal created it. There is a presumption of validity, and no further inquiry is needed unless there is good cause to believe it is invalid or has been revoked.[17] The UHCDA does not provide for recognition of non-US jurisdiction AHCDs.

13. Has your jurisdiction ratified The Hague Convention on the International Protection of Adults 2000? If not, are there any plans for your jurisdiction to do so in the near future?
The Hague Convention on the International Protection of Adults 2000 would be ratified at the federal level and AHCD are governed by state law.

14. Is there any publicly available guidance on the law and procedure concerning powers of representation in your jurisdiction?
There is widespread free information available from public sources on AHCD and the appointment of an HCS. The UHCDA includes an optional AHCD form.[18] Each individual state's Secretary of State office or Department of Public Health and Human Services have forms and instructions available to download.

Aging with Dignity, a US non-profit organisation, publishes an Advance Medical Directive entitled "Five Wishes".[19] This user-friendly form is distributed, free of charge, by faith-based communities and senior service organisations.

Physician's offices, hospitals and other medical providers have their own forms available if the individual has not executed an AHCD or if the AHCD is not current.

Notes

1 The UHCDA uses the term 'Advance Health-Care Directive' which is used here.
2 UHCDA, Section 3(a)(1).
3 *Ibid*, Section 3(a)(2)(A)–(B).
4 *Ibid*, Section 3(a)(2)(C).
5 *Ibid*, Section 4(a) and (b)(1)(A)–(C).
6 *Ibid*, Section 5(c).
7 *Ibid*, Section 12.
8 A plenary guardian is a guardian of the person and property.
9 UHCDA, Section 8(e).
10 *Ibid*, Section 8(a)–(d).
11 Several states with an AHCD Registry: Arizona, California, Rhode Island, West Virginia, Louisiana, Idaho, Montana, Nevada and North Carolina.
12 UHCDA, Section 15(a).
13 *Ibid*, Section 15(b).
14 *Ibid*, Section 15(d).
15 *Ibid*, Section 6.
16 *Ibid*, Section 26.
17 *Ibid*, Section 16.
18 *Ibid*, Section 11.
19 See www.fivewishes.org.

About the authors

Stephen Alexander
Partner, Mourant
stephen.alexander@mourant.com

Stephen Alexander is a partner, advocate and the practice leader of Mourant's Jersey litigation practice. He regularly advises on a wide range of multi-jurisdictional commercial disputes, with a particular focus in the areas of contentious private wealth and trust matters, partnership and investment fund disputes and corporate liquidations and reorganisations. Stephen is qualified in England and Wales, the Cayman Islands and Jersey.

Stephen is actively engaged in Jersey's business community and is the chair of STEP in Jersey. He also sits on the legal and regulatory committee of the Association of Restructuring and Insolvency Experts, the STEP Main Committee and Technical Sub-committee. Additionally, he sits as a standing member of the Law Society of Jersey committee, the body which regulates the legal profession in Jersey. He regularly delivers training sessions to the Jersey financial services industry and onshore firms.

Fraser Allister
Partner, Bedell Cristin
fraser.allister@bedellcristin.com

Fraser Allister is an international private client attorney at Bedell Cristin, specialising in all aspects of Cayman Islands and British Virgin Islands wealth structuring. He is a council member of STEP Cayman Islands and sits on its Regulatory and Legislative Committees.

Fraser is a contributing author to the Cayman chapter of *International Trust Precedents* (Sweet & Maxwell) and the British Virgin Islands and Cayman Islands chapters of *Private Trust Companies: A Handbook for Advisers* (Globe Law and Business, 2023). Fraser regularly speaks at conferences and other events on international wealth structuring.

Sherlynn G Chan
Partner, Deacons
sherlynn.chan@deacons.com

Sherlynn G Chan is the head of the family, mental capacity and vulnerable client practice at Deacons. She is a leading lawyer in mental capacity law and a seasoned family and private wealth lawyer. Sherlynn is a fellow of the International Academy of Family Lawyers and chairperson of the Mental Health Law Committee of the Law Society of Hong Kong. She is also the co-chair of STEP Hong Kong's Mental Health, Elderly and Capacity Law Sub-committee.

In addition to being a frequent speaker on family and private wealth matters both internationally and in Hong Kong, Sherlynn is the author of *A Practical Guide to Mental Health Law* in Hong Kong, published by Hong Kong University Press.

Sherlynn and her team won the "15th Annual STEP Private Client Awards – Vulnerable Client Advisory Practice of the Year" and is a finalist in the 19th Annual STEP Private Client Awards in the same category. They continue to serve the needs of vulnerable clients and their families.

Yue-En Chong
Founder, Bethel Chambers LLC
cye@bethelchambers.com

Yue-En Chong is the founder of Bethel Chambers LLC, a full-suited Singapore law firm providing both corporate and litigation services to clients. He holds an LLB from the National University of Singapore, an LLM from Cardiff University (Social Care Law) and a Master of Counselling degree from Monash University.

Yue-En personally specialises in cross-border probate, mental capacity law, estate planning and family law. He is also a professional deputy and donee (attorney) and has represented high-net-worth international families in this role.

At STEP, Yue-En is the current global chair of the Mental Capacity SIG Steering Committee. He is also the chair of the GRP Working Committee. As part of the GRP project, Yue-En frequently participates in discussions with national governments and local advocacy groups emphasising the need for laws to be enacted allowing everyone to have the freedom to make their own LPA/EPA.

Emily Deane
Technical counsel and head of government affairs, STEP
emily.deane@step.org

Emily Deane is technical counsel and head of government affairs at STEP, and is an internationally qualified private client lawyer. She has practised as a private client and trust solicitor in the United Kingdom, Bermuda and the Cayman Islands specialising in wills, property, tax planning, estate administration, onshore and offshore trusts and litigation.

Emily joined STEP in 2016 leading the policy team in relation to trust and estate-related issues. She informs public policy and promotes best practice in the private client industry, working with global regulators, lawmakers and stakeholders.

Farah Deba Mohamed Sofian
Partner, Wong Lu Peen & Tunku Alina
farah.deba@wlpta.com.my

Farah Deba Mohamed Sofian is a partner at Wong Lu Peen & Tunku Alina with over 30 years of experience in legal practice. Spearheading the inheritance and succession planning team, she led to broaden the legal firm's corporate, estate dispute resolution and real estate practice to offer estate planning services, which include trust and business succession and collaborative practice solutions.

Having accumulated over three decades of industry expertise, she serves a diverse portfolio of clientele ranging from individual private clients (from all walks of life, Muslims and non-Muslims included) to corporate institutions, not limited to trust companies, financial institutions, cooperative societies, family businesses, philanthropic and non-profit organisations. She customises *Shariah* and civil law estate planning solutions for local Malaysians and foreign residents. She also provides Labuan IBFC solutions for private wealth clients.

Farah is the current STEP Malaysia branch chair, a registered mediator with the Bar Council Malaysian Mediation Centre and a trained collaborative practitioner.

Sandra Duerden
Partner, Mourant
sandra.duerden@mourant.com

Sandra Duerden is a partner in Mourant's Guernsey litigation practice. She is an English-qualified solicitor and a Guernsey advocate with over 17 years' experience at Mourant. She is fluent in English and French and has a good knowledge of German and Lingala (being of Congolese heritage).

She specialises in commercial litigation and contentious trusts disputes and has a particular interest in commercial or trust disputes involving private international law aspects and cross-border disputes (particularly those which raise issues of jurisdiction and enforcement of foreign judgments).

Sandra primarily acts for fiduciaries or beneficiaries in complex, often multi-jurisdictional, trust litigation. She is a skilled liaison for clients in European countries including Switzerland, Monaco and Luxembourg and her French legal background also gives her insight into those aspects of Guernsey law which are based in Norman law. Sandra also regularly assists financial institutions and fiduciaries in commercial disputes and advises clients on the scope of their regulatory duties.

Joel Evans
Trainee, Mourant
joel.evans@mourant.com

Joel Evans is a trainee in Mourant's litigation team based in Jersey. Prior to joining Mourant, Joel worked at CEDR and the Beijing office of a leading Chinese law firm where he worked on various international arbitrations and cross-border disputes.

Kelly Greig
Partner, Blick Rothenberg
kelly.greig@blickrothenberg.com

Kelly Greig is chair of STEP Worldwide and a dual-qualified solicitor (non-practising) and chartered tax adviser specialising in international issues affecting private clients. Kelly is a private client partner at Blick Rothenberg which acts for high-net-worth individuals and corporate entities in structuring their affairs for future succession.

Kelly spent many years on the England and Wales panel of deputies – made up of those who are experts in mental capacity and acts as the person of last resort for those lacking capacity – and she has experience in financial abuse of the vulnerable as well as untangling complex legal issues for those lacking capacity.

Martin Haanen
Director and senior trust adviser, Castle Trustees Ltd
martin.haanen@castletrustees.co.nz

Martin Haanen is a TEP, director and senior trust adviser with Castle Trustees Ltd in Dunedin, New Zealand. Martin has more than 30 years' experience with trusts, estate and asset planning. He is a registered legal executive and has a master's in entrepreneurship. Martin was in the army and worked for the justice department. He also spent some time in the insurance industry and community mental health. He has been a court trustee with the Official Assignee's office and worked for various statutory trustees. He has acted as court-appointed property manager dealing with subject persons adjudged mentally incapable.

Martin is a board member of STEP's international Special Interest Group on Mental Capacity. He has a particular focus on intergenerational wealth transfer and the increasing risks we all face with an ageing population. Martin sees a power of representation as a fundamental way to lessen a client's risk, not just regarding the client's financial affairs, but also their personal care and welfare.

Nour Harb
Senior associate, Tindall Gask Bentley Lawyers
nharb@tgb.com.au

Nour Harb has been working exclusively in succession law since 2018. Nour's areas of expertise include all facets of estate planning, administration and litigation. Nour is a member of the Law Society of South Australia's Elder Law and Succession Committee and is also a succession law tutor at the University of Adelaide. Nour's interest areas include trusts, equity and superannuation.

Gilly Kennedy-Smith
Partner, Mourant
gilly.kennedy-smith@mourant.com

Gilly Kennedy-Smith heads up the award-winning trust and private client team in Guernsey at Mourant and has several years of experience in both London and offshore. She has been on two secondments to trust companies, which has provided practical experience of the issues facing the advisory team. She brings over

18 years' experience of working with international ultra-high-net-worth individuals, trust companies, family offices and independent financial advisers on the establishment, restructuring and management of family asset holding vehicles as well as estate and succession planning, with a focus on achieving private wealth objectives by thoughtful planning and governance. While her clients are global, she has particular experience working with Middle Eastern, Swiss and UK-connected clients.

Gilly is a member of STEP and sits on the Guernsey branch Technical Committee. She is also a tax technician and member of the Association of Tax Technicians. In 2024, She was appointed International Correspondent for *Private Client Business*, the leading journal for those involved with private client work. Gilly is also a Guernsey Advocate and has litigated in the Guernsey Court.

Ian Lebane
Vice president, tax and estate planner, TD Wealth
ian.lebane@td.com

With over 30 years of estate, trust and taxation experience, Ian Lebane has spent his career actively focused on providing holistic and comprehensive estate planning solutions to individuals, families and businesses, often consulting on complex issues. Ian has been a member of the Ontario Bar since 1990 and was in private practice focusing on estate planning and taxation until 1994, when he achieved his Master of Law in Taxation. From 1994 to 2006, Ian held various positions with the Law Society of Upper Canada related to lawyer training and accreditation in the areas of estates, trusts and taxation.

In 2007, Ian joined TD Wealth, Wealth Advisory Services as a will and estate planner, where he advises clients on the structure of their wills and often assists in setting up trusts, which can be particularly important considerations for beneficiaries with special needs. Ian works closely with clients and their outside advisers to implement strategies that will best help meet their unique circumstances. Ian is an experienced professional who will work with clients every step of the way to help them and their families progress towards achieving the goals and dreams they share.

Ian is the current branch chair of STEP Toronto; a board member of STEP Canada; and also chairs the STEP Canada Tax Technical Committee.

Andrew Miller
Partner, Bedell Cristin
andrew.miller@bedellcristin.com

Andrew Miller specialises in all aspects of Cayman Islands and British Virgin Islands (BVI) international wealth structuring for individuals and financial institutions. He is past chairman of STEP Cayman; the co-chairman of the STEP Cayman Legislative Committee, a founding board member of the STEP LatAm Conference and the STEP Cayman International Wealth Structuring Forum; a member of the International Tax Planning Association and the International Academy of Estate and Trust Law, an overseas member of the Chancery Bar Association and a fellow of the American College of Trust and Estate Counsel.

Andrew is the editor of the STEP Directory Cayman Section and contributes the Cayman Section of *International Trust Precedents*, the BVI section of International Succession Law and the BVI and Cayman sections of *Private Trust Companies: A Handbook for Advisers* (Globe Law and Business).

Timothy Morton
Consultant, Glass Goodwin
tmorton@glassgoodwin.com.au

Timothy Morton was admitted as a legal practitioner in 2011 and has worked solely in wills and estates law since 2010. His practice covers wills, estates, probate, estate litigation, tax law and equity litigation. Tim has been a committee member of the Elder Law and Succession Committee of the ACT Law Society since 2012. He presents seminars for a wide range of legal education topics within his areas of practice. He is passionate about learning and sharing what he learns with his peers.

Martina Moscardi
Senior partner, Caldara & Associati
m.moscardi@caldaraeassociati.it

Martina Moscardi – lawyer and partner at Caldera & Associati – has over 20 years of experience in the field of protection and transmission of private person wealth by legal tools like trusts, family agreements and other civil law instruments. Martina strives to take a problem-solving approach to practice and bring a constructive touch to clients' needs. Her work particularly relates to cross-border issues regarding inheritance and beneficiaries' rights and any other matter with international nuance. She is also currently devoted to mental capacity issues and diminishing capability regarding transmission of wealth and protection of beneficiaries' rights.

Martina has been an active member of STEP since 2005 and served as deputy chair of the local branch – STEP Italy – in whose running she is deeply involved. At STEP Global, Martina is the current deputy chair of the Mental Capacity SIG Steering Committee.

Martina was the first professional member in Italy and first woman professional in the STEP continental Europe area to win the STEP Founder's Award for Outstanding Achievements. She was also awarded the Award of the National Bar Association scholarship in EU Law and Regulations for young lawyers. As a general commitment, Martina acts in favour of non-profit associations.

William Ostick
Senior associate, Mourant
william.ostick@mourant.com

William Ostick is a senior associate in the international trusts and private client practice. He assists with a broad range of international trusts and private client issues. He advises trustees, high-net-worth individuals and family offices in achieving their objectives when it comes to wealth structuring, succession planning and trust and foundation set-up and administration.

William also assists high-net-worth individuals with any objectives they may have in the British Virgin Islands and the Cayman Islands, whether that be in conjunction with, or separate to, their needs in Guernsey. William works with several institutional trust companies on an ongoing basis, providing advice in relation to their powers, duties and responsibilities as fiduciaries. He also assists with the drafting of various instruments to give effect to the exercise of those powers.

Anthony Partridge
Partner, Ogier
anthony.partridge@ogier.com

Anthony Partridge specialises in all aspects of non-contentious and semi-contentious private trust and estate matters, wealth structuring for high-net-worth individuals, institutional trustees and family offices together with all related regulatory work and cross-border succession matters. He has particular expertise advising executors, beneficiaries and onshore counsel in relation to obtaining grants of probate, letters of administration and resealing foreign grants in the Grand Court of the Cayman Islands.

Anthony is the current chair of the Cayman Islands branch of STEP and has been a long-serving member of Council for many years. He also served as student liaison officer for the jurisdiction. Anthony is a member of the Cayman Islands Legal Practitioners Association and is a notary public in and for the Cayman Islands.

Shelley Rhoads Perry
Co-founder and CEO, Senior Advocacy Group
sperry@senioragroup.com

Shelley Rhoads Perry is co-founder and CEO of Senior Advocacy Group. The Naples-based firm provides fiduciary and lifecare management solutions for vulnerable adults and their families. Shelley and her team serve as agent under power of attorney, healthcare surrogate, independent trustee and personal representative, and also provide a full array of life-care management services.

She is a trust and estates attorney who has also held senior fiduciary planning and administration positions in a multi-family office and corporate trust department, in addition to practising in a boutique estate planning law firm. She has extensive experience in trust and estate administration as both an attorney and administrator, and is committed to assisting individuals and families dealing with the issues surrounding diminished capacity.

Shelley is a founding member of the STEP Digital Asset Global Special Interest Group and has also served on the STEP Mental Capacity Global Special Interest Group Steering Committee. She was an adjunct professor at Ave Maria Law School Estate Planning Clinic and is currently a member of the Professional Fiduciary Council of Florida's executive board. She speaks and writes on a variety of topics related to fiduciary services and vulnerable adults.

Leah Sewell
Barrister, Chalfont Chambers
leahsewell@chalfont.com.au

Leah Sewell was admitted as a legal practitioner in 2002 and worked as a solicitor in New South Wales (NSW) until April 2024. She specialised in wills and estates and was an accredited specialist in wills and estates law in NSW. Since 2022, Leah has been a member of the STEP Mental Capacity Special Interest Group. In May 2024, Leah was called to the NSW Bar, where she continues to work in the area of wills and estates and general equity.

Jason Tian
Senior partner, Shanghai Landing Law Offices
jie.tian@landinglawyer.com

Jason Tian is a founding partner of Landing Law Offices and head of the cross-border family and inheritance team in the firm. He was admitted as an IAFL Fellow in July 2022 – the third in mainland China. He is a long-term affiliate member of STEP.

Jason's legal practice covers services, mostly on behalf of foreign clients from outside China, such as cross-border estate planning and administration, family trusts, inheritance, insurance, international divorces, guardianship and custody, real estate, cross-border investments and foreign exchange control in China.

Claire van Overdijk KC
Senior counsel, Carey Olsen Bermuda
claire.vanoverdijk@careyolsen.com

Claire van Overdijk KC is senior counsel in the dispute resolution and litigation team and trusts and private wealth team at Carey Olsen Bermuda. She has extensive court experience in the fields of commercial and civil litigation, contentious and non-contentious trust and estate disputes and regulatory disputes. As a specialist in the resolution of complex disputes, Claire's practice is principally contentious extending to advocacy, strategic expertise and tactical advice in domestic and multi-jurisdictional high-value litigation.

As an expert in private international law, she is also well equipped to advise on cross-border elements that arise in these fields. Claire's client base is predominantly comprised of global businesses, financial institutions, public bodies, trustees, beneficiaries, settlors, protectors, private individuals and families.

In her spare time, Claire serves as panel chair for the Bermuda Human Rights Tribunal and the Bermuda Mental Health Tribunal. She is immediate past chair of the STEP Mental Capacity Global Special Interest Group and a full member of STEP. She has been called to the Bar of England and Wales and the Bermuda Bar.

Margaret Walsh
Partner, Sheil Solicitors LLP
margaretwalsh@sheilsolicitors.ie

Margaret Walsh joined Sheil Solicitors in 1987 and became a partner in 1991. Her extensive experience in recent years includes representation of local authorities and private clients in a variety of property transactions; commercial and residential conveyancing, retail landlord and tenant and all ancillary matters for private clients; acting for builders and developers of housing schemes, mixed developments, holiday home schemes, office and business parks, project management from site acquisition, through planning and construction to setting up appropriate legal structures and sales of units; and wills, taxation and estate planning.

Margaret is a serving member of the Law Society Advisory Committee on Probate Administration and Trusts, is currently a member of the Law Society's Mental Health Law and Capacity Task Force, is a full member of STEP and of Solicitors for the Elderly Ireland. She is editor of *Irish Conveyancing Precedents* (Bloomsbury Professional Limited).

Kevin J Winters
Associate, Brodies LLP
kevin.winters@brodies.com

Kevin J Winters is an associate in the personal and family team at Brodies LLP in Glasgow. Kevin deals in all aspects of private wealth law: the creation, administration, and wind-up of trusts; the drafting of wills and powers of attorney; and UK personal tax and estate planning and administration. He has a special interest in advising on matters where there is an international dimension and is frequently involved in advising on UK estate planning and administration where there is a cross-border element.

Kevin publishes in leading professional and scholarly journals including *Taxation, The Journal of the Law Society of Scotland* and *British Tax Review*. He is a full member of STEP.

About Globe Law and Business

Globe Law and Business was established in 2005. From the very beginning, we set out to create legal books that are sufficiently high level to be of real use to the experienced professional, yet still accessible and easy to navigate. Most of our authors are drawn from Magic Circle and other top commercial firms, both in the United Kingdom and internationally.

Our titles are carefully produced, with the utmost attention paid to editorial, design and production processes. We hope this results in high-quality publications that are easy to read and a pleasure to own.

In 2021, we were very pleased to announce the start of a new chapter for Globe Law and Business following the acquisition of law books under the imprint Ark Publishing. Our law firm management list is now significantly expanded with many well-known and loved Ark Publishing titles.

We are also pleased to announce the launch of our online content platform, Globe Law Online, which allows for easy access across firms. Details of all titles included can be found at www.globelawonline.com. Email glo@globelawandbusiness.com for further details and to arrange a free trial for you or your firm.

We'd very much like to hear from you with your thoughts and ideas for improving what we offer. Please do feel free to email me at sian@globelawandbusiness.com. Happy reading and thank you for your time.

Sian O'Neill
Managing director
Globe Law and Business
www.globelawandbusiness.com

Milton Keynes UK
Ingram Content Group UK Ltd.
UKHW051816031124
450528UK00004B/10

9 781837 230372